Jumpstart
Your Career

Jumpstart Your Career

ESSENTIAL STEPS TO A BRILLIANT FUTURE

PHILIPPA LAMB AND NIGEL CASSIDY

BBC ACTIVE

Educational Publishers LLP trading as BBC Active
Edinburgh Gate
Harlow
Essex CM20 2JE
England

First published 2006

The right of Philippa Lamb and Nigel Cassidy to be identified as authors of this Work
has been asserted by them in accordance with the Copyright, Designs and Patents Act,
1988.

ISBN: 0 563 52002 7

Commissioning Editor: Emma Shackleton
Project Editor: Jeanette Payne
Copy Editor: Patricia Burgess
Designer: Kevin O'Connor
Senior Production Controller: Man Fai Lau

Printed and bound by Ashford Colour Press Ltd, UK

The Publisher's policy is to use paper manufactured from sustainable forests.

Contents

Introduction

'Nothing is really work unless you would rather be doing
something else.'

J. M. Barrie (1860–1937)

If you want a better job, this book is for you.

There are lots of reasons why you might want to do something else.
Maybe you can't see a rewarding career path ahead of you, or you're working
ridiculous hours, or underpaid, or stuck with a boss who doesn't appreciate
you. Perhaps you're returning to work after time out caring for children,
studying or redundancy, and you don't know where to start. Or maybe
you just feel ready for a change. You're bored at work and longing to do
something more satisfying.

Whether you've made up your mind to make a move or it's just an idea
you're thinking about, this book will guide you on your way.

Work plays a big part in life, and it should do more for you than just pay
the bills. There's a whole world of exciting careers out there – this book will
show you how to become part of it.

HOW THIS BOOK WILL HELP YOU

Changing what you do for a living can be an exciting prospect. It can also seem like a daunting and difficult thing to do. You may be thinking about doing it because you want to, or because you feel you don't have any choice. Either way, this book can help you to:

- **Take an objective look** at what your work situation is right now and why you're not happy with it.

- **Think clearly** about all the practical issues you need to consider before you decide to make a career move.

- **Understand** yourself and what you can offer an employer.

- **Discover** what sort of work would satisfy and stimulate you.

- **Learn** how the working world is changing and what that means for you.

- **Find out** about a wide range of retraining options.

- **Research** jobs that could suit you.

- **Present yourself** in the most effective way.

- **Make a positive impression** when you start your new job.

- **Manage your career** effectively in future so that you won't end up in a job you don't enjoy again.

Jumpstart Your Career is a very straightforward book: no jargon, no complex theories, just practical advice about how to make a start on a fresh career path. We've kept it short and accessible so that it's easy to find the information you need. You can start at the beginning and read the whole thing, or just dip into the chapters that focus on areas in which you're particularly interested, such as interview technique or what employers are looking for.

At various points in the book you will find exercises that will help you to consolidate what you've read. They're well worth doing, but you'll still get a lot out of the text if you decide to skip them. You can always come back to them later if you want to.

◼ Why now is the time to make your career move

- What we do for a living has an enormous impact on how and where we live, the people we meet and the amount of time we can spend on partners, family, friends, travel and outside interests.

- A good job gives you a sense of satisfaction and self-worth which plays a big part in making you feel happy and contented. A bad job can take the edge off the sunniest day.

- The average person in the UK spends about 40 hours of every week working, and that doesn't include travelling time or all those extra hours we put into thinking about work. Most of us will continue doing that until we're 65, and many will carry on for far longer.

So isn't it about time you found a job you really enjoy? Life's too short to waste on anything less.

If you are in the wrong job, the good news is that you don't have to stay there.

Chapter 1
Time to make a move?

In this chapter you will find:

❏ Job satisfaction

❏ Is the job the problem?

❏ Work matters

Do you have days when you have to force yourself to get up and go to work – and by mid-morning you really want to go home again? It may be only mid-April, but you've already used up a year's worth of sick leave. You find it hard to keep motivated. You feel you could do your job standing on your head, and your mind wanders constantly.

Or maybe you feel as if you're drifting aimlessly because you fell into your current role almost by accident. You'd like to retrain or make a radical career change, but you don't know where to start (even though you have a sneaking feeling that the longer you put off making a move, the harder it's going to become).

Perhaps you need work that fits better around caring responsibilities, or maybe you'd like to 'downshift', go part time, or assemble a 'portfolio' of jobs to fit round other activities that are important to you.

It could be that you're in the employment market because you don't get on with your boss or your work colleagues, or you may be feeling unsettled by the possibility of redundancy.

Does any of that sound familiar? If it does, you're probably in the wrong job. But the good news is that you don't have to stay there.

■ Why your job no longer satisfies you

Discontent at work can take many forms. Research funded by the Economic and Social Research Council found that job satisfaction in the UK is declining slightly. According to the studies, it's not that we have unrealistic expectations, or don't want to knuckle down to daily employment, it's because we're fed up with excessive workloads, 'robotic' jobs and a lack of scope for personal initiative.

Eavesdrop on a typical group of office workers chatting around the water cooler and the chances are that someone will be saying something like this:

I can't live on this salary.

Other people I know doing this sort of work earn far more than me.

My workload is ridiculous – I'm stressed out.

Every day is the same – I never learn anything new.

They never give me promotion.

Why doesn't my boss use my skills?

There's no future for me here.

I'm always late picking up the kids from school.

Why doesn't this place offer decent childcare?

I can't stand the people in my department.

They won't reduce my hours.

I want to spend less time on the road.

Why can't I work from home sometimes?

I need to work flexitime.

Commuting is getting me down.

Unhappiness at work arises when you and the job your boss expects you to do are no longer a good fit. Problem areas often include:

- Skills
- Salary
- Values
- Freedom of action
- Status
- Hours and leave
- Conditions
- Organizational culture
- Promotion prospects

Repeated surveys suggest that, at any one time, as many as half of Britain's workers are saying that they want to change jobs within two years. Yet the reality for many is that inertia – or fear – will rule, and they will stay in a role they dislike rather than venture into the unknown.

Even worse, others may all but leave their job mentally, though they continue to turn up for work every day. This is an especially dangerous strategy, since it's the dead wood that will be the first to be pruned when management next swings the axe. If you have a choice, it is far better to go at a time of your own choosing – unless, that is, you are in line for a generous payoff, in which case you'll need to plan accordingly.

Alternatives to jumping ship

Before you storm into your boss's office and demand your P45, take a cool look at your present work situation. Maybe, instead of jumping ship, what you need to do is to turn round your existing employment to suit you better.

Might you be so wrapped up in your current responsibilities that you haven't considered seeking a different role with your present employer? If the firm is large enough, could you move to another department? Might you ask to take on more – or fewer – responsibilities, or retrain for a new role?

Is it worth trying to persuade your boss to give you a pay rise or a promotion? Do you have abilities that are under-used or unappreciated – skills that could enrich your job if only you were able to put them to better use?

■ Is the job the problem?

It's worth bearing in mind that the root of many problems we experience at work can actually lie elsewhere in our personal or home life. We may not even realize how unresolved troubles may be taking a toll on our performance or effectiveness. If you're thinking about a career move because you're miserable, you need to make sure it's your job that's making you feel that way. It can be easy to think that different work will make you happy. It might, but even the most fantastic job isn't going to do that for you if there are other things in your life that are making you depressed. For instance, are you worried about:

- Your relationship with your partner?
- Family difficulties?
- Your finances?
- Children?
- Health?
- Addiction to alcohol, drugs or tobacco?
- Weight problems?

If any of these strikes a chord, you should seek some outside help. Your GP, for example, will be able to advise you about health, fitness or addiction issues. The Citizens Advice Bureau (**www.citizensadvice.org.uk**) can help with problems concerning debt, benefits, housing, the law, discrimination, employment, immigration and consumer issues. The charity Relate offers advice, relationship counselling, sex therapy, workshops, mediation, consultations and support face-to-face, by phone or through its website (**www.relate.org.uk**). For other problems you might consider approaching an experienced counsellor (**www. bacp.co.uk**) or life coach (**www.coachfederation.org**). Sometimes all it takes to help you see your way forward is to share your difficulties with a good friend.

This isn't the book you need to read if you're in difficulties with relationships or personal issues beyond work. Whatever they are, you need to tackle them *before* you think about changing your career. If you don't, there's a real danger that you'll put a lot of effort into finding a new job only to realize that your life hasn't changed fundamentally for the better and you'll end up even more demoralized than before.

■ Work matters

Although most of us have to work for money, what we do for a living connects us with others and should, ideally, reflect our personal values and strengths.

It's crucially important to achieve a good balance between work and home life. Professional and personal satisfaction, along with good health, are the ingredients we all need for a sense of wellbeing. So we owe it to ourselves and our families to get it right. All jobs have their drawbacks and irritations, but if you're not happy in the one you're doing, it's well worth making the effort to discover, or even create, a job that will allow you to live a life that suits you better.

You have already taken the first step to a new career by reading this far. So, once you have taken stock of where you are job-wise, you can start thinking about what you'd ideally like to get into, what opportunities are actually out there, and how you can start putting these two things together.

■ Key points

- Job discontent is often caused by excessive workloads, 'robotic' jobs and a lack of scope for personal initiative.
- Many people remain in roles they dislike because they fear venturing into the unknown.
- Job dissatisfaction can make you ill, and feeling unappreciated can make you angry and irritable.
- Rethinking your career should allow you to live the life you really want outside work, as well as making the time you spend in the workplace actively enjoyable.

If you are ambitious, or seek career fulfilment, what is it that stands in your way of getting to the next level?

Chapter 2
Why do I feel I'm being left behind at work?

In this chapter you will find:

❑ Career change

❑ Ageism

❑ People skills

❑ Learning from your mistakes

❑ Can you have it all?

Not so very long ago, signing up with a large firm, such as a bank or a local factory, was practically a ticket to a job for life. Yet now, within a single generation, the prospect of secure and varied employment with one employer – with a decent pension thrown in – has pretty well vanished. For most of us, what lies ahead is not so much a 'job for life', as a 'life of jobs'.

If you had expected to stick with that same old firm until retirement, it comes as a shock to discover that your job is on the skids, or that you will have to make a move if you want to get on.

■ Career change has become commonplace

Thanks to new technology and digital communications, there's been a revolution in how people choose to live, spend their money and occupy their leisure time. This has had a profound effect on the goods and services that companies are able to sell profitably. In turn, this has had an impact on the kind of people these firms need to employ.

The worlds of work and business are moving ahead so rapidly that career change has become entirely commonplace. Hardly any job feels secure.

For the last 25 years, competitive pressures on organizations have forced them to be constantly on the lookout for new ways of cutting their labour costs. This has led to their farming out accounts, IT, catering and other office functions, with the inevitable toll on jobs. Computer technology allows the administrative, technical and secretarial back-up once provided by armies of support staff to be provided by far fewer people.

A decade or so ago, companies were taking on large numbers of people to answer phones in customer call centres. Increasingly, these jobs are being 'outsourced' and sent overseas. Offshore contractors are taking on ever more complex functions such as designing software and financial management.

At the same time, firms have taken to employing many more workers on temporary or fixed-term contracts – people they can get rid of quickly if business is slack or the economy turns down.

Financial software, databases and internet-based computer tools are now in everyday use on office desktops, and the prospects for workers who are not up to speed with these are increasingly limited. It's invariably when you try to change jobs that you discover gaps in your knowledge of IT. These are gaps that may have to be plugged (see Chapter 11) before applying for job interviews.

People in support roles of any kind are especially vulnerable. Until the whirlwind of technological change actually hits your own office or department, you might not even have realized that your work could be 'non-core'. This term is applied to those in jobs that are ultimately a cost to the boss because they do not involve bringing in new business or creating the actual product or service that is sold at a profit.

■ They think I'm too old...

In most jobs your age ought not to be a barrier to continued, fruitful employment. Older workers can call on many years' detailed knowledge of products, suppliers and customers. And if their children have flown the nest, most will have fewer family commitments to distract them. Unfortunately, the real worth of older workers is not always appreciated by companies until they 'oversack' during a crisis. They then discover that none of their younger, cheaper new recruits has the right know-how, and there's nobody on hand to coach the new staff. Customers become unhappy, orders are lost and productivity may sink.

It's certainly true that older staff are more expensive to employ if they have risen through the ranks to senior positions. They are also sometimes regarded as resistant to change, difficult to mould and more likely to take time off for illness. The perception is that younger workers are more flexible, better with computers, and readier to stay late or do whatever it takes to get on. So if you are over 40 and in the job market, ensure that your good health and liking for an active life are made crystal clear on your CV and job application form.

If you're an older worker and finding it difficult to move into a more challenging or better-paid role, it may be worth actively seeking out firms with an established track record of employing people over 50 as part of their overall mix of workers. You can obtain useful, up-to-date advice on this from organizations such as Age Concern (**www.ageconcern.co.uk**) and the Employers Forum on Age (**www.efa.org.uk**).

Fortunately, times are changing. For a start, the pool of potential younger workers is shrinking and simple demographics are reversing the trend to force older workers into early retirement. In any case, people will need to work longer to build up a bigger pension pot.

From October 2006 EU age discrimination rules will become part of UK employment law. For the first time, job advertising and redundancy policies can no longer favour younger (or, indeed, older) workers. As well as that, if you reach 65, you can ask to stay on in your job, and your employer will have only limited grounds to turn down your request.

■ They say I'm not good with people

While we are all driven mad by helplines that don't help us and home deliveries that never arrive, we are all demanding and getting better service from private and public organizations than ever before. As a result, the staffing of those organizations has had to change. People who were once cosily hidden behind the scenes handling paperwork or business processes are being forced on to the customer front line.

While some people relish dealing with the general public, others find it a pain. If your problem-solving, communication or social skills are not highly rated, this could be the time to brush them up (see Chapter 11). Without realizing it, almost anyone can develop a 'negative attitude' at work – something you don't want to take with you to your next job.

■ Time to start being honest with yourself

Job blues often brew from what may at first seem like a single event. Perhaps you have unexpectedly lost out on a promotion, or had a row with your manager. Perhaps you were made another job offer and turned it down, and are now regretting your decision. Almost overnight you have a job crisis on your hands.

Deciding what to do is tricky because inevitably your emotions will get in the way. For example, you might be doing a well-paid, prestigious job, yet also be in despair at your long hours or the amount of time you have to be on the road. While you might like to take things easier, you can hardly bear to contemplate giving up the status that goes with the job.

■ Can you have it all?

The notion of 'having it all' – an entirely fulfilling home life *and* a stellar career – is beguiling. But it is also misleading.

If you want to aim for the top, you should be under no illusion that you will have to deploy every ounce of talent, ingenuity, salesmanship and connections to get there. True success at work often demands punishing hours and unremitting hustle. The alternative is to choose not to join in the game, remaining happier, though poorer, by staying out.

Most of us will strive for a middle way between these two extremes, aiming to better ourselves at work as far as we can in line with our personal commitments. But you do need to work out your priorities.

Ask yourself the question 'What am I working for?' If it is really just the money, this will influence what kind of job you should go for. Do you simply want work close to home that pays enough to meet the bills? Or are you thinking that you'd be prepared to put up with long hours and hassle if you could earn far more than you do at the moment? If job satisfaction is important to you, what kind of job would allow you to maximize the elements of your work that you like best? If you are ambitious or seek career fulfilment, what is it that stands in your way of getting to the next level? (For more on what motivates you, see Chapter 5.)

■ Career planning starts with a crisis

Being forced out of a comfortable phase of your working life and into another can be extremely stressful. Yet, as many people who have been through career traumas will tell you, a more satisfying working life can await you if you start to consider what it is you really want.

Losing a job can feel very frightening, and few people relish change. But isn't the prospect of never doing the things you want far worse?

■ Key points

- Often, what lies ahead is not so much a 'job for life', as a 'life of jobs'.
- Be cautious about 'non-core' work in which you are a cost to the business.
- Older workers having trouble finding a job can actively target firms known to favour mature employees.
- Consider carefully if you have developed any negative attitudes and pledge to leave them behind you when you make your job move.

Our future success as a country depends on people starting or helping to grow businesses that will provide sources of employment, competition and new ideas.

Chapter 3
New jobs, new ways of working

In this chapter you will find:

❏ There's no substitute for skills

❏ Welcome to part-time Britain

❏ One person, several jobs

❏ Working from home

How do you fancy becoming a ubicomp technologist, or a bioinformatics specialist? The titles might sound weird, but these are just two of the new kinds of job the City & Guilds examination board (**www.city-and-guilds. co.uk**) predicts will be among the professions of the near future.

'Ubicomp', by the way, is a combination of 'ubiquitous' and 'computer'. The idea is that people may soon be employed working out how to embed tiny computers into homes and everyday objects. For example, a larder could be equipped to re-order goods as soon as stocks become low.

'Bioinformatics' is the vast area of research opened up by the discovery of the human DNA sequence. Chemistry and biology are expected to come together in a new field employing large numbers of people to process and compare huge quantities of information.

Now, you may say, this is all very interesting, but it's way beyond me and far outside my particular field. Well, it's true that we won't all be designing computer chips, but it's a fact that, no matter where we live, new technology has already transformed the jobs marketplace in the UK. Dozens of familiar jobs are fading away, and new ones are taking their place.

It's hard to believe that the World Wide Web was invented as recently as 1989. So integral has it become to life and work that it seems to have been around forever. It is estimated that eight out of ten office workers use email and information technology in their jobs, and that around half of manual workers use a computer at home, and make increasing use of IT in the workplace.

■ Middle-ranking jobs are melting

What perhaps wasn't foreseen about advancing technology was that it would start kicking away rungs on the career ladder. In other words, computers are taking the place of people who used to be employed doing middle-ranking skilled jobs – anything from assembling cars to doing secretarial work.

At the lower end of the job market there are usually plenty of jobs going in areas such as retailing and customer service. At the top end there's strong demand for highly experienced professionals and deal-makers. What's getting harder – if you don't have skills or the right education – is finding places where you can start at the bottom and steadily work your way up the ladder. Organizations are sometimes described as 'flat', which means that most people are working at approximately the same level or grade. This, in turn, means that there are fewer opportunities for promotion.

■ There's no substitute for skills

In short, if we want to progress, we will need to keep updating our skills throughout our working life. So this may be just the time to think about courses or retraining, and you will find everything you need to get started on that in Chapter 11.

No one can predict exactly what the working world will look like in even ten years' time. What we can be sure of is that the successful enterprises of the future will be those with the most skilled, creative, innovative and enthusiastic workers.

Our future success as a country depends on people starting or helping to grow businesses that will provide sources of employment, competition and new ideas. Larger firms will also need people who can spot opportunities and adapt their strategies to changing circumstances. Inevitably, some organizations will streak ahead and others will fall by the wayside. It's this kind of change or 'churn' that results in people having to change their jobs more often.

■ No job lasts forever

Given the information so far, it follows that you are unlikely to be on your last job hunt. Like it or not, it's your employer who will determine how long a job lasts. And some bosses today do seem to show little commitment to individual workers. This may come as a shock if you have previously worked for someone who frequently praised or acknowledged your contribution. That's why it's always best to pick work you think you will enjoy for its own sake. Any recognition you then receive for your achievements will be an unexpected bonus.

■ Goodbye manufacturing, hello services

The most obvious change in Britain's employment opportunities has been the long-term decline in manufacturing. It is widely forecast that almost 2 million extra jobs will be created in service industries between now and 2010.

A huge growth area is personal services. Rising incomes, fewer people living in traditional family units and most of us living longer, will all create a demand for people to keep us well fed, looking good and feeling physically and mentally fit. We'll need more hairdressers and personal trainers, and visit ever-larger numbers of therapists for anything from body waxing to dietary guidance. This is good news for those with practical skills because there's no risk of all those pampering jobs being exported overseas. And when did you last hear about an out-of-work plumber?

Worried that you might end up without a job at all? Take heart. Recent history suggests that your chances of staying unemployed are falling. In 2001 less than five per cent of the working population were without a job, compared to 11 per cent in 1986. By 2011 it's also estimated that a million more women will have joined the UK workforce.

■ Welcome to part-time Britain

Looking back, the twentieth century may come to be regarded as the last era of the full-time, permanent job. By contrast, the twenty-first century may prove to be the century of part-time jobs and self-employment. Already almost a quarter of the entire UK workforce works part time. A high proportion of such jobs are concentrated in catering, care and office work; far fewer are in areas such as construction and manufacturing.

In the UK in 2004, some 83 per cent of part-time workers were women. While male part-time workers are gradually increasing, men tend to go part time when they are combining education with work or seeking to cut down their hours as they approach retirement age.

Companies are employing growing numbers of part-time, temporary or seasonal staff. They rely on importing workers to carry out specific tasks on special contracts, and are increasingly reliant on self-employed consultants. These are part of today's army of 'knowledge workers', many of whom may once have had full-time posts with the same or similar organizations. Your present employment could be coming to an end, but there might just be a ready market for your skills if you are able to apply them to a wider range of customers or other businesses.

In particular, employers are hiring temporary or 'interim' managers to complete one-off projects, or to cover for staff absence. Such jobs are not just stopgaps: they look great on your CV and can sometimes allow you to gain hands-on experience in a new field or business sector.

■ Pressures employers can't resist

When it comes to finding suitable workers, some employers are tapping a ready supply of people from beyond these shores, notably eastern Europe. Many are happy to take jobs in such fields as farming, catering, transport or the building trade, sometimes working for slightly lower wages than may be the current going rate. Good employers will do all they can to retain their existing workforces, yet the willingness of people from lower-waged countries to do such work to a high standard can have an impact on both pay and job opportunities.

■ One person, several jobs

It could be that some of the work you might be interested in doing in the future may not be conveniently packaged in the form of a 'proper' full-time job. Temporary employment contracts may soon be as common as part-time ones. Employers only want to employ expensive labour when it is really needed.

More people will have a 'portfolio' of two, three or even four jobs that they do during the course of a week. Some might do this out of choice, others out of financial necessity. If one employer cannot offer you sufficient work to fill a week or the whole of a year, it makes perfect sense to look for additional jobs elsewhere.

Building up a track record and progressing with 'flexible' firms may take some persistence. You will have to use your initiative to find out for yourself what opportunities might be out there, and work hard to get your talents noticed. Proper on-the-job training may not be available, so you might have to swallow your pride and ask for some unpaid work experience, or act as a low-paid 'gofer' to get yourself started.

In their book *Licensed to Work* (1995), authors Barrie Sherman and Phil Judkins analysed official employment trends published by the Organization for Economic Cooperation and Development. They believe that self-employment and freelance work will increase so much that they will become almost the norm.

■ Why workers have to deliver

Like it or not, almost as soon as you start a job your productivity and effectiveness may be judged against that of others. For example, how much business do you bring in? How many customers do you deal with, or how many problems can you solve for your employer in a day?

Don't take such scrutiny personally. It's a simple fact that inefficient companies are unable to cover their costs and produce a profit, so it's sound business sense to keep track of employees' efficiency. One of the main reasons for this is globalization, the technological revolution that enables information and goods to travel much faster than ever before. Customers can scour the entire country – in some cases the entire world – to find the best deal. Increasingly, the old divisions between the people who make the decisions and the people who carry out the actual work are fast disappearing. Being able to type and handle a computer is no longer a skill in itself – it's a basic requirement. You make the sale – you also have to prepare and send out the necessary paperwork. The stark truth is that those who are unwilling to work flexibly and add to their skills are at much greater risk of losing their job.

■ Working from home

A few years ago, it was predicted that up to half the workforce would soon be giving up commuting and operating from home instead. The trend is certainly gathering pace, but not as quickly as was once forecast. Working from home can be lonely (many people miss the opportunity for a good gossip with workmates), and you do need to be organized. It's important to have a clear dividing line between domestic and office areas, even if your workplace is just a corner where work materials can remain undisturbed. In order to make the psychological separation, some people claim that they have to leave the house, then walk back in to go to work. Remember too that while you need self-discipline to work at home, you also require the discipline to stop what you are doing and pay attention to family members.

Generally, home working is an option more likely to be taken by people who are already established in their field.

When we talk about working from home, also known as 'teleworking', we tend to think only of those who are self-employed. In the UK today, more than 5 million people already spend some time working at home, and this number is expected to rise. If home working or being more of your own boss appeals to you, it might be a good idea to target companies that offer an element of flexible working. This could involve anything from varying your hours or start-time to spending some of the week at home as your work tasks dictate. This kind of existence can give you a little more personal control of your own working life. It may be, for example, that you work far more efficiently in the late evening, so it makes sense for your employer to let you work then, rather than forcing you to perform when you may be preoccupied with other things.

British Telecom (BT) is one of the largest organizations to have experimented with home working. In fact, 70,000 of its staff now work flexible hours. But firms are not offering this style of working out of the goodness of their hearts. Not having to house so many staff in offices is said to be saving BT £180 million a year.

Working from home, either for yourself or as a paid employee, can seem like a very appealing option – no more train fares or battling through the rush-hour traffic; no more work shirts to iron; just the convenience of a home office and the freedom to take a quick trip to the supermarket or pick up the kids from school whenever you need to. Well yes, but homeworking doesn't suit everyone, and the most common difficulty that people run into is loneliness. You might relish the idea of not having to work alongside irritating colleagues, but working on your own, day in, day out, can be isolating.

ARE YOU SUITED TO WORKING FROM HOME?

Here's a lighthearted quiz to help you discover whether working from your own home might be a good option for you. Be honest, tick the answer (a, b or c) that describes most closely your response to each question. Once you have worked through the questions, you can score your answers and get the results at the end.

1. At my current place of work I like to:
   a. Break up the day by chatting with whoever is around.
   b. Have colleagues congregating at my desk for gossip over coffee.
   c. Prioritize my day and keep focused so that I complete essential tasks.

2. When I am seeking information from people, I try (if possible) to:
   a. Speak to them in person – there's no substitute for direct contact.
   b. Use email – it's quicker and easier.
   c. Telephone people – I prefer to hear their voices.

3. **When it comes to praise for my own work performance:**
   a. I can live without it – I'm my own best critic.
   b. I like to be praised from time to time.
   c. Positive feedback and criticism are important to me.

4. **When the dirty dishes have piled up at home and there are no more clean cups:**
   a. I feel guilty, but wash up just enough to get by.
   b. I leave the kitchen quickly and shut the door.
   c. I reach for the dish mop and get it done quickly.

5. **Most of my friends tend to be:**
   a. Mates from work.
   b. A mixture of people from work and elsewhere.
   c. Friends from outside the workplace.

6. **As an employee, I would say that:**
   a. I work most effectively running my own projects.
   b. I am known as a team player.
   c. I sometimes need a nudge to do my best work.

7. **My own home is:**
   a. A good base, as long as I can get out for some time every day.
   b. My haven – there's nowhere else in the world that makes me feel more relaxed.
   c. The ideal place to live and work, as long as I can escape once in a while.

Work out your score

Give yourself the following number of points, depending on which answer you chose:

1. a 5; b 15; c 0
2. a 10; b 0; c 5
3. a 0; b 5; c 15
4. a 5; b 10; c 0
5. a 10; b 5; c 0
6. a 0; b 5; c 15
7. a 10; b 0; c 5

- **If you scored 0–25:** You may well be ideally suited to working from home. You are self-directed and like to keep on top of tasks so as to get the job done as efficiently as possible.

- **If you scored 26–50:** You could feel isolated and face some initial challenges in opting out of the traditional workplace, but it might still be the answer if you work through your reservations and focus on the work tasks in hand.

- **If you scored more than 50:** It's probably not a good idea to give up your day job until you have thought more about whether you could motivate yourself without the security of colleagues and tasks set by others.

Let the sun shine in

If your financial needs rule out working anything less than a five-day week, perhaps 'sunlighting' could make you a little less office bound. This system allows you to spend four days being paid to do your job, and the fifth on pursuing other career interests. Your additional occupation might not be as well paid, but perhaps it could offer you more personal satisfaction. And what's in it for your boss? Well, he or she might like the idea of saving a fifth of your salary.

Hot, cold and lukewarm jobs

Few of us are likely to choose our next job simply because it's forecast to be a hot job of the future. Even so, it is fascinating to discover which employment fields are among those forecast to see high growth rates between now and 2010.

Jobs on the up

Airline pilots and crew

Artists and entertainers

Beauty therapists, chiropodists and
    masseurs

Cable installers and service
    providers

Computer security consultants

Electronic engineers

Golf professionals

Parking attendants

Personal and home health carers

Plastic surgeons

Plumbers
Prison officials
Private police and security staff
Private tutors
Psychologists
Research scientists and technicians

Specialist computer programmers
Specialist doctors
Systems analysts and designers
Tax advisers
Telecommunications sales staff
Travel consultants

Jobs holding steady

Bus and lorry drivers
Construction workers
Craft workers
General practice doctors
Government sector managers and
    administrators
Hospital ancillaries

Personal secretaries/assistants
Pharmacists
Supermarket checkout staff and
    shelf-stackers
Teachers and lecturers
TV and press journalists

Jobs on the decline

Administrators
Bank and building society assistants
Book-keepers
Car dealers
Clerical and filing staff
Currency and stockmarket dealers
Engineering staff
Estate agents
Farm workers
Health service managers
Insurance brokers
Labourers

Light assembly workers
Low-level computer jobs, such as
    data-inputting
Metalworkers, skilled
Middle managers
Milk roundsmen/women
Newspaper delivery boys/girls
Postal workers
Printers
Railway staff
Telephonists
Warehousing and storage jobs

■ Key points

■ Traditional jobs in offices and industry are fast being replaced by new ones, most of them in service industries requiring skilled use of IT, or providing people with services in their own homes.

■ Part-time, freelance and contract working will become almost as common as full-time employment.

■ More jobs will offer a measure of 'home working'. These may suit more established workers, as they offer a greater degree of control over your working life.

What's important is to make a distinction between your earning ambitions and how much you actually need to stay afloat. What you earn over and above that is the icing on the cake.

Chapter 4
Practical matters to think about

In this chapter you will find:

❏ Money

❏ Your monthly spending

❏ Budgeting

❏ Cutting costs

❏ Deciding what you *don't* want

Daydreaming about changing your job is one thing but actually doing it is quite another. So before you go any further, consider all the practical implications that moving into a new job might have for you (and the people close to you, such as partners or children) and work out how you will deal with all of them when the time comes.

■ Money

Salary is by no means the most important factor when it comes to career choice. Well, that's what numerous research studies tell us; nonetheless, we all have bills to pay, so money is a significant issue for most of us.

You may be looking for different work simply because you have to earn more to meet all your financial commitments. On the other hand, you might not mind taking a pay cut if it means that you can shift into a more satisfying role. Either way, if you're thinking of moving into an entirely different field or retraining (see Chapter 12 for more on this), you might have to make do with a lower income for a while before you can match or exceed your current income.

What's important is to make a distinction between your earning ambitions and how much money you actually need to stay afloat. And staying afloat depends on your personal circumstances and the level of comfort you feel you can't do without. What you earn over and above that is the icing on the cake.

Working out how much you need to bring in is simple. You can calculate where you stand financially either by filling in your current monthly outgoings and income in the following tables, or completing one of the many online versions such as the Business Link personal budget spreadsheet (**http://www. businesslink.gov.uk**) or the Financial Services Authority budget calculator (**http://www.fsa.gov.uk/consumer**).

Your monthly spending	Now	Future
Income tax and other salary deductions		
Mortgage/rent		
Council tax		
Home and contents insurance		
Home maintenance		

Your monthly spending	Now	Future
Water rates		
Fuel and power bills		
Phone bills (landline and mobile)		
Other loan repayments		
Other insurance (medical/life/income protection)		
Regular savings		
Childcare		
School/tuition fees		
Financial support for children not living with you		
Financial support for other family members		
Food and non-alcoholic drinks		
Alcohol		
Tobacco		
Clothing and footwear		
Dry cleaning		
Household goods		
Toiletries/beauty products		
Motoring		
Fares		
Going out		
Holidays		
Hairdressing/other personal services		
Membership fees		
Other outgoings		
Total:	£	

If you want to find out roughly how much you spend over an entire year, simply multiply your total by 12. You can also divide by the number of hours you work each year to get a general idea of how much you need to earn per hour to cover your current costs. Our example below uses 2000, which is based on a 45-hour week.

Total spending each month:	£2083.00
Multiplied by 12 months:	£25,000.00 per year
Divided by 2000 hours:	£12.50 per hour

Your income	£
Salary or earnings from self-employment	
Regular contributions from family/former partners	
Child benefit and tax credits	
Other state benefits	
Interest from savings accounts	
Income from shares, unit trusts or other investments	
Pensions from former employers or pension plans	
State pension	
Other	
Total:	£

Multiply by 12 to find out your total income for this year and see how it compares to your annual spending.

If you're hoping to raise your earning potential by changing your job (or your outgoings will rise in future due to expenses such as a bigger mortgage, school fees or increased pension contributions), you might like to create a 'future personal budget'. Fill in the 'Future' column of the spending chart, making realistic estimates of what you will be spending in each area in future.

The benefits of budgeting

- Once you have calculated how much you need to earn every month, you will know which career options and individual jobs are unsuitable, simply because they won't pay you enough to meet your basic needs.
- If you've created a personal budget forecast, you will know what minimum level of salary you need to look for in your career choices and searches for actual jobs.
- You now know exactly where your money goes each month.

■ Cutting your costs

Unless you're living on a subsistence wage that covers only your basic needs, such as housing, food, clothing and transport, you could probably reduce your monthly outgoings if you needed to.

You may decide it's worth forgoing a few luxuries if it means that you can take up a career that really inspires you. On the other hand, you may feel that the whole point of going out to work every day is that it allows you to spend money on the things you enjoy.

If you do want to cut your costs, a careful look through your personal budget will quickly show you areas where you should be able to scale back your spending. Economize on entertainment, eating out, ready-prepared meals and luxury foods, clothes and holidays and you may be surprised how much money you can save.

If it turns out you will need to make savage cuts in your household spending, there are various organizations that can give you advice about how to plan or restructure your biggest outgoings.

Debt restructuring

Citizens Advice Bureau – www.citizensadvice.org.uk and www.adviceguide.org.uk (follow the links to 'Your Money')

Consumer Credit Counselling Service – www.cccs.co.uk

National Debtline – www.nationaldebtline.co.uk

Mortgages and remortgaging

Citizens Advice Bureau – www.citizensadvice.org.uk and www.adviceguide.org.uk (follow the links to 'Housing')

Financial Services Authority – www.fsa.gov.uk/consumer (follow the links to 'Mortgages')

Pension planning

Pension Service (part of the Department for Work and Pensions) – www.thepensionservice.gov.uk

Financial Services Authority – www.fsa.gov.uk/consumer (follow the links to 'Pensions')

■ Don't bury your head in the sand

For most of us, what we earn plays an important part in the decisions we make about our careers, so think hard about the part money plays as far as you're concerned. The answer will depend on your personal circumstances and your personality. If your desire to change career is all about earning more money, for whatever reason, plan your search on that basis. If pay isn't a big motivator for you, think hard about what *is* before trying to identify possible lines of work (that's what the next chapter is all about).

■ Your domestic situation

Taking a new job – especially a full-time one – will have implications for other people in your life. These may be financial, emotional and/or practical.

The very thought of your making a job change can be unsettling or even frightening for other family members. If you're prepared to turn your back on a perfectly good job, what will you want to do next? Far from being enthusiastic about your career-change ambitions, your partner's reaction may be positively hostile – particularly if you're the main earner, or you share family responsibilities or financial commitments, such as a mortgage. Children too can become anxious when faced with a parent who suddenly wants to do something unexpected.

The practical issues for people close to you will often be time-related. If you're going to spend the majority of your waking hours job-hunting or retraining, who's going to do the school run/weekly shop/cleaning/caring for elderly dependents? Will you still have time to coach the school football team/sing in the local choir/keep up your voluntary work commitments? Will you suddenly stop finding time to devote to your partner?

If you're considering working or starting up a business from home, you'll need to consult the rest of your household about how that might work. Can you find a suitable workspace that you can use daily without disrupting everyone else who lives with you? What hours will you work? Will you tie up the only phone or the family PC for 24 hours a day? There's a whole raft of considerations to take into account (see Chapter 10).

Try not to exclude those closest to you from your career search. Broach your plans carefully: friends and family can be invaluable sources of encouragement and support, and are less likely to be alienated and negative if you keep them in the loop. Listen to what they have to say and be patient. You've done a great deal more thinking about the situation than they have, and you're the one who's going to have all the fun of a fantastic new job.

WHAT HAVE YOU LEARNT ABOUT WORK SO FAR?

Soon we're going to be exploring what gets you motivated and bouncing through the office door with a spring in your step. But first let's take a look at the flipside: what bugged you most about the jobs you have done in the past and – if you're currently working – the job you're doing now?

In my next job I don't want...
Make a list of all the things you *don't* want to put up with in your next job. These might include:

An unappreciative boss	Lack of proper rewards
No clear career path	Long or inflexible working hours
No security	An unpredictable workload
Repetitiveness	Obligatory teamwork
Obligatory isolation	Unsociable colleagues
Managing others	High level of personal responsibility
No decision-making	A lengthy commute
Time away from family	A large, faceless employer
A small company	

Add any other pet hates you can think of, then take a cool, appraising look down your list.

When you think about it, some of the things listed will be bigger issues for you than others, so you might want to reorganize your list, putting the things you find most exasperating or demotivating at the top, and ranking your other dislikes accordingly.

When you've finished, the dislikes at the bottom of your list won't be things you feel very strongly about, but the ones at the top could well be 'deal breakers' – in other words, issues you feel so strongly about that you would refuse a job if they featured very highly.

The list might look like this:

> Irregular working hours
> Low pay
> Poor promotion prospects
> Unsociable colleagues
> Long commute to work
> Old-fashioned offices

For the person who wrote this list, irregular working hours and low pay would cause them such major domestic problems that they wouldn't be prepared to take even a really exciting job if it meant putting up with them. On the other hand, even though it would be nice to have a shorter commute to work and more stylish offices, they're not issues that would stand in the way of them taking a job they really liked the look of.

■ Be realistic

If you've ended up with a very long list of things you are determined not to tolerate in your next job, bear in mind that setting too many restrictions will inevitably narrow your options. Ask yourself whether your reasons for disliking those aspects of working life are practical or emotional. For example:

■ Do you respond badly to being closely supervised whatever the circumstances? Or do you just resent being over-supervised by your existing line manager? In other words, will this be a fundamental issue for you in *any* job, or simply something that doesn't work well in your current one?

■ Is access to training genuinely essential to you, or would you be prepared to take responsibility for your own training needs out of office hours through night classes or distance learning?

■ Are you quite certain that you never want to work for a small organization? Does this feeling come from having had a bad experience with one particular small firm where the management didn't look after you properly?

■ Will a longer commute *always* be out of the question for you? Could your reluctance to travel far be more to do with childcare or being on time for a school run? Might it be possible for you to reorganize things with help from family or friends? Perhaps you could talk to a potential employer about flexible hours or working only during term time.

This is a useful process to go through because it begins to give you a clearer idea of why the jobs you have had in the past may not have turned out as you had hoped.

When you begin to assess the pros and cons of alternative careers, keep your list of workplace dislikes in mind, and don't forget it when you go for job interviews. Review your list beforehand and use it as a basis for questions to ask about both the specific role on offer and the wider organization. If the issues on your list blighted your working life in the past, you don't want to find yourself putting up with the same things in the future.

■ Key points

■ Work out how much you need to earn before you move on to thinking about alternative careers.

■ Be aware of the impact your decision to change career might have on people close to you.

■ Analyse your working life to date: what was wrong with it?

A job that genuinely inspires you and satisfies you can make a long-term contribution to how much you enjoy life.

Chapter 5
What drives you?

In this chapter you will find:

❑ What do you want out of a job?

❑ Motivation

❑ Past, present and future

❑ Ambitions

When you've made up your mind to find different work, the temptation to start looking for a new job straight away is almost irresistible. The obvious thing seems to be to surf a few job sites online, apply for a few posts you like the look of in the newspaper, ask around among your friends, or maybe go off to see a recruitment agency. Before you know it, you've got a couple of interviews lined up and you feel as if you're really making progress.

This is what most people do, and some find good new jobs that way. But the question to ask yourself is whether a job you find like that is likely to be the *best* job you could possibly get.

Working out whether you have really landed a great job takes time. New offices, new colleagues and new tasks can be energizing for a while; it can take months to discover that all you've actually done is to swap one unsatisfactory job for another. All those familiar feelings of discontent and boredom creep back, and the realization dawns that you're still in a rut.

■ What do you want out of a job?

Whatever job we do, work plays a big part in our life. At the most basic level, it's something that fills our time week in, week out for years on end. For that reason alone it's worth finding an occupation that does more than pay the bills. Yet what we do in the workplace has a far wider impact on our life and well-being. Money should not be the only reward.

Career gurus like to use high-flown language to describe job satisfaction. They talk about jobs that 'make your soul sing' or 'show you the best person you can be'. If you're anything like us, you may have a hard time believing that you'll ever find a job that really does all that for you. But buried beneath such flowery descriptions there is something worth thinking about – which is that work can have an enormous impact on your happiness. A job that genuinely inspires and satisfies you can make a long-term contribution to how much you enjoy life. However content you may be outside work, it's difficult to feel completely happy if you're trapped in an unsatisfying career.

ANALYSE YOURSELF

To maximize your chances of moving into work that you find satisfying and enjoyable you first need to do a little self-analysis. What would a job need to be like to make you feel enthusiastic about doing it? What sort of management style from your boss would encourage you to produce the best work that you're capable of? What sort of organization would you flourish in? In other words, what motivates you?

Here's a list of job characteristics that commonly motivate or drive people at work. Take a look through it and add any others you can think of that are important to you.

My drivers	Importance ranking	My current job
Secure employment		
Good pay		
Good promotion prospects		
Status		
Having an efficient and competent superior		
Respect for me as an individual		
Being able to participate in the decisions that affect me		
Working by myself		
Knowing I will be held responsible for my own performance		
Freedom to make decisions		
Being able to problem solve		
Being commended when I do a good job		
Getting a performance rating so that I know where I stand		
Feeling my job is important		
Having control over others		
Influencing outcomes		
Variety in my work		
Opportunity for self-development and improvement		
Flexible working hours		
Not having to work long or irregular hours		
No pressure		
Having consistency in my job		
Opportunity to produce high-quality work		
Opportunity to do creative and challenging work		
Good physical working conditions		

My drivers	Importance ranking	My current job
Opportunities to use up-to-date technology and resources		
Getting along with colleagues		
Socializing with colleagues outside office hours		
Pensions and other fringe benefits		
Knowing what is going on in the organization		
My employer's contribution to the wider community		
Company willingness to let me spend time on community activities		
Agreement with employer's objectives		

Now consider which of the drivers in the first column on the list would play the biggest part in motivating you to do your best work. Choose the seven that you feel are most important, then allocate each of them a grade in the second column of the chart:

E = essential

I = important

D = desirable

Try not to rank all your chosen seven as essential or important or you won't get the best out of this exercise. Think hard about what you *most* want your work to offer you and how it should fit in with your family or other interests and responsibilities.

This exercise should leave you with a helpful list of essential, important and desirable features to look for from your next job. If they are present, you will feel more motivated to do the best work you can.

If you want to pin down some of the reasons why you're discontented in your *current* job, fill in the final column of the chart. Look at the seven drivers you've already picked out as essential, important or desirable. Does your present role offer you many of these drivers? You should quickly see where the mismatches are.

You can also use your lists as the basis for good questions to ask when you go for job interviews. For example:

- Whom would I be responsible for managing and whom would I report to?
- Do your staff at my level find that they need to come into the office at weekends on a regular basis?
- What sort of training would I receive and when?
- Where can you see me fitting into your organization in, say, three years?

If you enjoy doing online tests, you'll find dozens relating to motivation at work. For example, the graduate careers site **www.prospects.ac.uk** offers a self-assessment of skills, interests and motivators, while the Shell site **www.thebigtrip.co.uk/thebigtrip**, aimed at young, would-be entrepreneurs, helps you rate, among other things, your 'key personal values'. The American site **http://mentalhelp.net/psyhelp** is an entire self-help manual that includes a chapter on motivation.

So check those out, but meanwhile, try the following exercise.

PAST, PRESENT AND FUTURE

Write down the five most significant past events in your life, or any you have planned for the future. Don't think too long and hard about this – go with your first instincts. Once you've got your list, ask yourself what the events you have noted down indicate is important to you. Consider how you would like your work to interact with such life events in the future.

■ Be honest about your ambitions

Many people feel you have to be extremely ambitious to have a successful career. In fact, it's a common misconception that 'good' jobs are those that are 'senior' or 'high profile', while lower-level positions are always less desirable.

In reality, the best job for you is the one where there is a close match between what the employer expects and how much time and effort you are prepared to put into the role in return for your salary. If you're keen to make it to the top of the corporate tree, you'll be looking for a demanding and time-consuming job that will stretch your abilities and help you to make your next move up the management hierarchy. If, on the other hand, your main priorities lie with family, friends or outside interests, a good job in your terms may well be less testing, with shorter, more regular hours and fewer responsibilities.

This is an important issue, and you need to be clear in your mind about it. Would you rather impress people with a high-status, high-reward job, or find a less stressful role that allows you to create a happy balance between your work and the rest of your life? (There is no 'right' answer to this question, by the way – it all depends on what works best for you.)

Some people look to their work to identify or validate themselves as successful individuals. Others get that sort of reassurance from elsewhere in their life. We don't all want to end up as chief executives, and there's nothing wrong with being modest in your ambitions on the work front. A successful career move is one that makes you *happier*, not necessarily wealthier or more important.

So, when you go job hunting, don't forget those job features you marked as essential or important. These are big issues for you.

■ Key points

- Resist the temptation to start looking for a new job before you have worked out what motivates you to do your best work.
- Money can be an important motivator, but other aspects may be more important to you in your search for a new career.
- Be honest with yourself about how big a part you want your work to play in your life.

If you are clear in your mind about your skills and abilities, and understand how you tend to behave in given situations, you will find it much easier to identify careers where you can shine.

Chapter 6
What do you have to offer?

In this chapter you will find:

❏ Transferable skills

❏ Personality analysis

Your own particular blend of skills, experience and personality is what makes you better suited to some types of work than others. So the more you understand about that blend, the better. If you are clear in your mind about your skills and abilities, and understand how you tend to behave in given situations, you will find it much easier to identify careers where you can shine.

■ Analyse your skills

If you've been working for some years, you may feel you have a pretty good grasp of what your skills are. However, it's worth taking time to reassess them carefully as people often underestimate their own abilities.

Your 'transferable skills' or 'core competencies', as they're sometimes known, are the basic tools you use to do your job. The ones you use most will depend on the job you're doing at the time, and most of us find that expanding and honing our skills plays a big part in making our work satisfying.

How you use your skills depends upon your traits, and we'll get on to how you can identify your individual personality traits in the next chapter. For now, though, you just need to understand that being, for example, a workaholic is a trait, not a skill. It describes how you go about your work, not what you do to get a job done. The same goes for descriptions such as 'energetic', 'reliable', 'good under pressure' and 'a quick learner'. To put it another way, traits are *innate*, whereas skills require *will*.

Transferable skills

The basic abilities that you bring to any job are often divided by careers specialists into the following types:

- **Information-handling** – such as analysing data, computing, researching and editing.
- **Interpersonal** – such as managing, teaching, training and negotiating.
- **Creative and ideas-related** – involved in generating ideas, inventing concepts and solutions, creative writing and the arts.
- **Working with things** – such as operating specialist machinery, driving, and making and maintaining things.

Let's say you currently work as a teacher: it's easy to identify at least some of the skills you employ. They will certainly include:

Instructing

Supervising

Explaining

Planning

Researching

Monitoring

But in your dealings with pupils, colleagues and parents you might also employ skills such as:

Persuading

Negotiating

Problem-solving

Networking

Mentoring

Team-building

Collaborating

Spend ten minutes writing a list of the skills you use at work. It will come in handy when you start thinking about jobs.

Every so often, you'll see we suggest making lists of your skills, ideas, priorities and so on. You may be tempted not to bother, but creating these highly personalized lists is definitely worthwhile. Writing down your thoughts and conclusions will help you to think more clearly and rigorously (try composing an essay in your head if you don't believe us). Research has shown that people who write down their goals are more likely to achieve them.

■ Skills you may have overlooked

It's easy to overlook some of your skills, particularly the ones that may not be a direct part of your job. For example, working as a legal executive may involve using skills such as researching, analysing, explaining and negotiating. However, you may also be the person to whom colleagues turn for help because of your natural talent for developing others' potential. Maybe you're the one who always manages office reorganizations, or comes up with the most creative ideas for the Christmas party.

The skills you use daily in your dealings with other people play a vital part in how well you perform at work and what you have to offer potential employers. Think about what they are. Are you particularly skilled at persuading others? Resolving disputes? Spotting people who will work well together? Perhaps you have a talent for motivating people? Or helping them to solve problems?

You should analyse everything you do at work to form an accurate picture of the skills you have, not just the tasks you're directly paid to perform. Add them all to your list of competencies. And don't forget about all the skills you use in your private life, which could be put to use in the right job. Think about the roles you perform outside the office, such as:

Voluntary work

Organizing social events/outings

Itinerary planning your family holidays

DIY and home improvements

Fund-raising

Coaching a local sports team

What skills do you use – and enjoy using – when you are doing things in your own time? These are valuable transferable skills for you to add to your list and take into your new career. (And if you haven't started a list yet, re-read page 55 about why you need to do so.)

■ Test yourself

Online tests can be a helpful way to identify the skills you have to offer. You will find dozens of them on the web, but if you are unclear where to start, or short of time, check out **www.learndirect-futures.co.uk** or the very comprehensive US site **http://online.onecenter.org** to get you started.

■ Ask your friends

Pick three or four friends, family members or trusted colleagues and ask each of them (ideally over a quiet coffee or a drink) what they think are your greatest skills. (You may first have to explain the difference between skills and traits.) Try to resist interrupting, even if you disagree. The idea isn't to have a debate, but to form an impression of what others think you're capable of. This can be a very revealing exercise if they come up with skills you hadn't even thought you possessed.

■ Develop skills you can deploy anywhere

A university research team once analysed over 10,000 graduate recruitment advertisements in national newspapers. It found that recruiters valued, in order of importance, oral communication, teamwork, enthusiasm, motivation, initiative, leadership, commitment, interpersonal skills, organization and foreign language competence.

Other skills often found lacking in candidates of all ages included time management, communication, decision-making and problem-solving. Notice that these are all transferable skills. So no matter how dazzling your specific achievements, make sure you're able to demonstrate that you can apply the skills you have learnt to any situation your new job may throw at you.

■ Analyse your personality

We've talked about what drives you at work and how you can assess your own skills, but there's more to working out what makes you tick than that. Tens of thousands of other people have skills similar to yours, yet add your personality and life experience to the equation and you become an individual with a unique combination of attributes to use in your working life.

So how does personality fit into career planning? Research suggests that particular personality types tend to flock together at work. It's not a hard and fast rule, and there are plenty of exceptions, but if you were to analyse the sort of people who have become bankers, actors or potters, you would find that many of them share personality traits as well as skills.

Don't get too hung up on this theory because, clearly, we each have our own unique blend of personality, skills, aptitudes and experience. However, it is worth assessing your own personality because it can often highlight career opportunities that you might not have thought about before.

■ Personality tests

If you like the idea of doing personality tests or quizzes, you'll find dozens of them on the internet, ranging from the highly academic (you'll often have to pay, or at least register with the site, to do these) to the most simplistic (usually free). When you've got an hour it's worth trying out a few and comparing the results you come up with.

Bear in mind that this kind of self-analysis can produce very black and white results, and you can end up feeling boxed in by what the tests tell you about yourself. Use them as a guide to how you tend to behave, rather than a hard and fast assessment of who you are.

If you have not already visited it, one of the best places to start your online research is the careers section of the government-backed Learn Direct site **www.learndirect-futures.co.uk**. After registering, you can take online tests to identify your individual interests, values and skills. You can also check out **www.learndirect-advice.co.uk/helpandadvice/dmr/** for a helpful online test to tell you what sort of decision-maker you are and to receive a short personal profile.

You may well have heard of the Myers-Briggs Type Indicator® in connection with personality testing. This is one of the longest-standing and best-known methods used by specialists to measure personality. You'll have to pay a trained practitioner to conduct a full-blown Myers-Briggs analysis of your personality type, but you can do a mini online version at **http://tools. monster.com/perfectcareer** to get a flavour of how the theory works.

The Prospects site (**www.prospects.ac.uk**), which is aimed at graduates, has an exercise called 'Prospects planner' (under 'What jobs would suit me?'). In this you select the field you focused on in higher education and build up a personal profile from sections on skills, interests and motivations. The exercise software then matches your profiles with types of job.

The Careers Group at the University of London (**www.careers.lon.ac.uk/ SORTIT**) is also aimed at graduates. It offers useful self-knowledge exercises, listings of different occupations, and career-generating ideas.

The site **www.peoplemaps.co.uk** will give you a mini personalized report, including a potential employer's opinion of you.

If you prefer the idea of doing a personality test on paper, here's one for you to try.

WHO DO YOU THINK YOU ARE?

This test measures how you describe yourself, and the results will help you to think creatively about the sort of work you might like to move into. There are no right or wrong answers. There is also no time limit, but most people take about 30 minutes to complete the test.

Here's what to do. Look down the list of words on the left-hand side of the table. Taking each of the 90 words in turn, circle the ✔ if this is most like you, or the ✖ if this is least like you. If you are neither one extreme nor the other, circle the N.

The easiest way to score your results is probably to make a numbered list on a separate sheet of paper and tick, cross or write N next to each number as you go through the table in the book.

	Description	Most like you	Least like you	Neither
1	Calm	✔	✖	N
2	Cynical	✔	✖	N
3	Sociable	✔	✖	N
4	Confident	✔	✖	N
5	Creative	✔	✖	N
6	Systematic	✔	✖	N
7	Trusting	✔	✖	N
8	Relaxed	✔	✖	N
9	Talkative	✔	✖	N
10	Cooperative	✔	✖	N
11	Practical	✔	✖	N
12	Methodical	✔	✖	N
13	Enthusiastic	✔	✖	N
14	Imaginative	✔	✖	N
15	Persevering	✔	✖	N
16	Happy-go-lucky	✔	✖	N
17	Patient	✔	✖	N
18	Easygoing	✔	✖	N
19	Nervous	✔	✖	N
20	Passive	✔	✖	N
21	Disorganized	✔	✖	N
22	Easily upset	✔	✖	N
23	Shy	✔	✖	N
24	Absent-minded	✔	✖	N
25	Challenging	✔	✖	N
26	Emotional	✔	✖	N
27	Undisciplined	✔	✖	N
28	Assertive	✔	✖	N
29	Self-sufficient	✔	✖	N

	Description	Most like you	Least like you	Neither
30	Factual	✔	✘	N
31	Reserved	✔	✘	N
32	Accepting	✔	✘	N
33	Precise	✔	✘	N
34	Retiring	✔	✘	N
35	Anxious	✔	✘	N
36	Artistic	✔	✘	N
37	Stable	✔	✘	N
38	Sceptical	✔	✘	N
39	Down-to-earth	✔	✘	N
40	Temperamental	✔	✘	N
41	Cold and distant	✔	✘	N
42	Chaotic	✔	✘	N
43	Diplomatic	✔	✘	N
44	Composed	✔	✘	N
45	Innovative	✔	✘	N
46	Dominant	✔	✘	N
47	Fun-loving	✔	✘	N
48	Detail-conscious	✔	✘	N
49	Outgoing	✔	✘	N
50	Pragmatic	✔	✘	N
51	Critical	✔	✘	N
52	Quiet	✔	✘	N
53	Sensitive	✔	✘	N
54	Flexible	✔	✘	N
55	Meticulous	✔	✘	N
56	Humane	✔	✘	N
57	Self-assured	✔	✘	N
58	Spontaneous	✔	✘	N
59	Volatile	✔	✘	N
60	Lively	✔	✘	N
61	Open-minded	✔	✘	N
62	Conscientious	✔	✘	N
63	Outspoken	✔	✘	N
64	Realistic	✔	✘	N
65	Competitive	✔	✘	N
66	Unruffled	✔	✘	N

	Description	Most like you	Least like you	Neither
67	Rigid	✔	✘	N
68	Confrontational	✔	✘	N
69	Inward-looking	✔	✘	N
70	Impulsive	✔	✘	N
71	Tense	✔	✘	N
72	Deep	✔	✘	N
73	Inventive	✔	✘	N
74	Informal	✔	✘	N
75	Balanced	✔	✘	N
76	Hands-on	✔	✘	N
77	Charitable	✔	✘	N
78	Participating	✔	✘	N
79	Exacting	✔	✘	N
80	Tolerant	✔	✘	N
81	Original	✔	✘	N
82	Free-spirited	✔	✘	N
83	Sober and serious	✔	✘	N
84	Conceptual	✔	✘	N
85	Theoretical	✔	✘	N
86	Untidy	✔	✘	N
87	Self-reliant	✔	✘	N
88	Matter-of-fact	✔	✘	N
89	Restless	✔	✘	N
90	Active	✔	✘	N

© Psytech International – www.psytech.co.uk

How to score your answers

This takes a few minutes, so don't rush it. The results are organized into five grids, which represent five key areas. When you have scored the test, your results will show how you described yourself in each key area. For example, the first one shows your degree of extraversion – the extent to which your thinking is shaped by the world around you, rather than by your inner thoughts and reflections.

To find your score, work through each of your answers in turn, circling the number that corresponds to your response. For example, if you ticked word number 3 (Sociable), give yourself two points. If you put a cross, no points. If you answered 'Neither', give yourself one point. Once you have completed each grid, add up the total score of the numbers you have circled.

1. EXTRAVERSION

Description	✔	✘	Neither	Description	✔	✘	Neither
3	2	0	1	47	2	0	1
9	2	0	1	49	2	0	1
41	0	2	1	52	0	2	1
13	2	0	1	60	2	0	1
16	2	0	1	69	0	2	1
23	0	2	1	78	2	0	1
29	0	2	1	83	0	2	1
31	0	2	1	87	0	2	1
34	0	2	1	90	2	0	1

Total points:_____

2. OPENNESS

Description	✔	✘	Neither	Description	✔	✘	Neither
5	2	0	1	61	2	0	1
11	0	2	1	64	0	2	1
14	2	0	1	72	2	0	1
24	2	0	1	73	2	0	1
30	0	2	1	76	0	2	1
36	2	0	1	81	2	0	1
39	0	2	1	84	2	0	1
45	2	0	1	85	2	0	1
50	0	2	1	88	0	2	1

Total points:_____

3. AGREEABLENESS

Description	✔	✖	Neither
2	0	2	1
7	2	0	1
10	2	0	1
18	2	0	1
20	2	0	1
25	0	2	1
28	0	2	1
32	2	0	1
38	0	2	1

Description	✔	✖	Neither
43	2	0	1
46	0	2	1
51	0	2	1
56	2	0	1
63	0	2	1
65	0	2	1
68	0	2	1
77	2	0	1
80	2	0	1

Total points:_____

4. STABILITY

Description	✔	✖	Neither
1	2	0	1
4	2	0	1
8	2	0	1
17	2	0	1
19	0	2	1
22	0	2	1
26	0	2	1
35	0	2	1
37	2	0	1

Description	✔	✖	Neither
40	0	2	1
44	2	0	1
53	0	2	1
57	2	0	1
59	0	2	1
66	2	0	1
71	0	2	1
75	2	0	1
89	0	2	1

Total points:_____

5. CONTROL

Description	✔	✘	Neither	Description	✔	✘	Neither
6	2	0	1	55	2	0	1
12	2	0	1	58	0	2	1
15	2	0	1	62	2	0	1
21	0	2	1	67	2	0	1
27	0	2	1	70	0	2	1
33	2	0	1	74	0	2	1
42	0	2	1	79	2	0	1
48	2	0	1	82	0	2	1
54	0	2	1	86	0	2	1

Total points:_____

How to interpret your answers

Once you have a total score for each category, you can read off your results from the following sections. All you need to know is that:

0–11 is a low score
12–24 is an average score
25–36 is a high score

Let's see how you fared in each of the five categories.

1. EXTRAVERSION

If you are a low scorer, you are happy to work independently, away from the distraction of other people. You enjoy your own company and have little need for constant contact with others. It is likely that you will take a while to get to know new people and may slip into the background at social events. You are unlikely to require constant variety, change and excitement. You may prefer roles that involve independent work and not constantly having to meet and deal with new people.

If you are a high scorer, you greatly enjoy the company of others. Talkative, outgoing and sociable, you dislike being on your own for long periods of time. By nature lively and participative, you enjoy social occasions and are likely to take centre stage at parties and events. You actively seek variety and change, and need a high level of stimulation in order to avoid becoming bored. As a result, you may prefer roles that involve a high level of social contact, particularly if this involves initiating, developing and maintaining relationships.

2. OPENNESS

Low scorers are down-to-earth people who have their feet firmly planted on the ground. Your thinking style is realistic and practical, and you are inclined to reject theoretical approaches to problem-solving. You are more interested in learning practical skills and techniques that have immediate relevance. Preferring to focus on concrete issues, you are more concerned to get things working than to ponder why they work. As a result, you are likely to enjoy roles that involve solving real-life problems.

High scorers are inclined to think in abstract, theoretical ways. At times you may become so involved with your own thoughts and ideas as to lose track of practical realities. Being open to theoretical possibilities and unconventional ideas, you are inclined to bring a radical, innovative approach to problem-solving. You are likely to enjoy roles that provide opportunities for you to express your creativity and originality in a scientific, artistic or business context.

3. AGREEABLENESS

Low scorers are especially suited to roles where it is important to have a cool and questioning take on other people's behaviour. You are likely to be a little cynical, suspicious or sceptical, and may sometimes question other people's motives. As a result, you will not easily be taken in by flattery or praise. With practice, you may be able to train yourself to be less suspicious.

High scorers are trusting and kind-hearted by nature. You are quick to help those you see as being more needy than yourself and are inclined to give people the benefit of the doubt. However, others may sometimes take advantage of your goodwill. You are a good team player, suited to all roles that require building trusting relationships with others.

4. STABILITY

Low scorers are prone to mood swings and can be volatile, which can at times make life 'interesting'. You may be easily upset by others, or react badly to criticism, even if it is justified. You may have a tendency to worry about past failures. Stressful work is not likely to suit you, and neither is working long hours under pressure.

High scorers are emotionally stable, calm and composed, and not prone to mood swings. You generally cope well under pressure, and are unlikely to become tense, irritable, moody or upset by what others say. You could be well suited to roles that are emotionally challenging or involve working under pressure for long hours.

5. CONTROL

Low scorers tend to be spontaneous and impulsive, and comfortable with change. You are suited to roles that require adaptability and flexibility, and don't enjoy making detailed plans and schedules. You are unlikely to be particularly well organized or systematic in your work, and must guard against losing interest in tasks before they are finished. You may spread yourself across too many different jobs at once. You might be ill suited to roles that involve rigidly following set systems, procedures and rules.

High scorers on this scale pay attention to detail and display self-control and restraint. You are well organized and like to plan ahead carefully. Diligent and persevering by nature, you have a strong sense of duty. Once you have started a task, you probably feel compelled to see it through to the end. You feel comfortable working in well-structured environments. You might not be best suited to working in places with rapidly changing priorities and goals, where you have constantly to think on your feet.

■ Key points

- Transferable skills are the basic tools you use to do your job.
- Be careful not to overlook your less obvious skills.
- Your personality and life experience are important parts of what you have to offer potential employers.
- Similar personality types tend to flock together in different occupations.
- Personality tests can give you useful insight into how you behave at work.

Nowadays, employers want self-starters who are good collaborators, able to come up with good ideas and creative solutions with a minimum of supervision.

Chapter 7
What are employers looking for?

In this chapter you will find:

❏ How to present yourself

❏ Attitude

❏ Flexibility

❏ Diversity in the workplace

There's no big mystery about what employers are after: they're looking for good people. And the excellent news from the job-hunter's point of view is that they can't find enough of them. In a survey for the Chartered Institute of Personnel and Development (CIPD), 85 per cent of employers said that they were having difficulty in recruiting high-quality staff. It seems to be the same story year in, year out, regardless of the state of the job market. And when recruiters talk about 'high quality' they don't just mean the kind of exceptionally qualified candidates you might expect to be in short supply.

The universal complaint among employers is that they don't see anything like enough strong applicants for jobs of all kinds and at all levels.

■ Presenting yourself in the most positive light

Naturally, the lack of decent candidates does not mean that you can expect to get *any* job you want. Part of the reason that employers struggle to find good people is that they have to waste a lot of time wading through poor-quality or inappropriate applications. There's little point applying for vacancies that don't at least broadly match your skills and experience. You'll be lucky to get a rejection letter, let alone an interview.

If you want to move into a new career, you will need to find out as much as possible about the sort of people who are in demand in that field and set about equipping yourself to become one of them (see Chapters 11 and 12). Just as importantly, you will need to work out how best to present yourself and the skills and experience you *do* have in the most positive light (see Chapters 14 and 15). This is because most employers end up solving their recruitment problems by taking on the people who they believe have the most *potential,* even if they don't currently fit the precise requirements of the post they need to fill.

■ Essential skills

So what fundamental skills do most employers look for? According to the American academic Professor Lawrence Jones, whatever the nature of your job, you will need 17 'foundation skills' to do it as well as possible. The skills divide into four groups:

- **Basic skills:** reading, writing, mathematics, speaking, listening.
- **Thinking skills:** creative thinking, problem-solving, decision-making, visualization (imagining how a system might work by looking at a diagram).
- **People skills:** sociability, negotiation, leadership, teamwork, cultural diversity.
- **Personal qualities:** self-esteem, self-management, responsibility.

But which skills do employers rate as the most useful? When it comes to younger recruits they tend to look for basic skills, such as literacy and numeracy, and a positive attitude to work. In more mature workers bosses value more complex skills, particularly business awareness, self-management, communication and teamworking abilities, and problem-solving.

In the past employers looked for recruits with strong administrative and technical skills, and who were good at controlling other workers. But as you can see from the list above, nowadays they want self-starters who are good collaborators, able to come up with effective ideas and creative solutions with a minimum of supervision.

■ Attitude

In the past, filling a vacancy was all about a candidate 'fitting' the job. Recruiters wanted people who were qualified and skilled for particular tasks. It was a logical approach to recruiting at a time when the pace of change in the working world was slower, and people stayed longer in their jobs.

Now things are different. Clearly, employers still need to recruit people who can do the job effectively and be great staff managers. But they want something else as well: 'flexibility'. Indeed, this is now seen as a key component of competitive success. Organizations need to be in a position to make the most of the business opportunities and challenges they face. Without versatile staff, they can't be quick on their feet.

So what do employers mean when they say they want 'flexible workers'? Well, in general what they want is staff who:

- Are open to new ideas.
- Accept new ways of working easily and quickly.
- Are willing to learn new skills throughout their working life.
- Are prepared to work irregular hours.
- Are prepared to relocate for their work if need be.

Unfortunately for those who look for stability in their working life, the natural extension of a flexible workforce can be a workforce that employers have to pay for only when they want to use it – hence the growth in contract work and the use of freelance staff. According to the employers' organization the Confederation of British Industry (CBI), agency temps now make up five per cent of the UK workforce – that's about 700,000 people. Many of them are used to cover short-term staff absences, but the current trend is for agency assignments to last longer than in the past, and most of them now continue for more than six weeks.

■ Flexibility works both ways

If you have always been used to working the traditional hours of 9–5, it's worth remembering that flexible working practices don't just benefit employers. The widespread introduction of varied working hours has been generally good news for millions of employees, who now find it easier to balance their work with other personal commitments.

According to the CBI, 90 per cent of employers now offer their staff at least one form of flexible work. The most common is part-time working (now offered by 85 per cent of employers), followed by flexitime (39 per cent) and job-sharing (34 per cent). Unsurprisingly, it's the biggest organizations that tend to offer the widest range of flexible working arrangements. Yet smaller enterprises aren't that far behind. Of those with fewer than 50 staff, 80 per cent employ part-timers and 45 per cent offer flexitime, though small firms are less likely to have job-sharers on their books.

If flexible working is something you're looking for, you should also bear in mind that different job sectors tend to offer it in different forms. Flexitime is most widely available in banking, finance, insurance and professional services, where technology makes flexible working easier to manage and so-called family-friendly policies are widespread. Hotels, restaurants, retailing and manufacturing, on the other hand, are far less likely to offer flexible working because they habitually employ more shift, fixed-term and part-time workers.

Since 2003 employees with young or disabled children have had the legal right to request flexible working hours. Employers do not have to agree to it if they can make a business case for refusing you. Yet, according to the

CBI's research, only one request in ten is actually turned down flat, with small firms the most likely to agree.

The government is currently considering extending this 'right to ask' to other groups of employees. Encouragingly, the CBI found around a quarter of the bosses it questioned were at least willing to consider such requests from staff not currently covered by the legislation.

■ Diverse workforce

Shrewd employers understand the advantages of having a workforce that reflects Britain's diverse population. In fact, according to the CBI, three-quarters of employers now say that they can see a clear business case for diversity. Even if some are only paying lip-service to the whole concept, it's undeniable that work opportunities for those who don't fit the 'white, male' stereotype are greater than they have been. If you haven't been in the job market for a while, you may be surprised to discover how many employers are actively trying to find staff from minority groups.

A raft of legislation outlaws discrimination against job applicants on the grounds of sex, race, ethnic origin, disability, sexual orientation or faith. In 2005 it also became illegal to discriminate against candidates on the grounds that they are too young or too old.

The fact is that Britain's rapidly ageing population is already prompting many employers to reinvent their ideas about recruitment. For the remainder of your working life there will be fewer young people coming into the job market, so employers of every sort are already having to think more creatively about:

■ What sort of people they will be recruiting in future.
■ How they will need to change the way their organizations operate in order to compete in a more complex job market.
■ How individual jobs will need to change to appeal to job seekers who don't fit the traditional recruitment profile (for example, older workers, staff with disabilities, applicants from overseas, and so on).

This is all good news. Time and money are being invested in diversity programmes, staff wellness initiatives (helping employees with issues such as diet, exercise and medical advice), childcare facilities and even concièrge services (practical domestic help, such as collecting dry cleaning, organizing grocery shopping or sourcing reliable tradespeople). It's all evidence of a new attitude, and is on the rise in both the private and public sectors.

All organizations claim to be 'equal opportunity' employers nowadays. In reality, some are more equal than others. Do your research before you accept a job:

- Read what the website or corporate brochure has to say.
- Visit the premises and see for yourself who actually works there.
- Ask questions about the range of people on the staff.

Don't be misled by statistics such as '15 per cent of our staff belong to ethnic minority groups'. Ask what sort of work those people are doing. Are they executives or canteen staff?

■ Commitment

Hiring new staff is a time-consuming and expensive business for employers. According to a CIPD survey, the average bill ranges from around £10,000 to find a senior manager or director down to around £1,000 to recruit a manual worker. Finding suitable administrative, managerial and professional staff costs between £2,000 and £5,000 for each post filled, plus more time and money on induction and training.

Understandably, this means that employers usually prefer job applicants who say they will stay long term with the organization. They are often seen as having the edge over better-qualified candidates who give the impression of seeing the post as a short-term stepping-stone.

■ Honesty

Trying to find work in a new sector can be tough, and receiving a string of rejection letters might tempt you to wonder if stretching the truth a little about your skills, experience or job history might improve your chances. While it's only common sense to downplay your weaknesses and highlight your strengths, resorting to outright deception is a dangerous game.

When the CIPD surveyed employers last year they discovered that nearly 80 per cent of them *always* check references, and one in four of them had withdrawn a job offer that year as a result of a candidate lying or otherwise misrepresenting information in their application. Although anecdotal evidence suggests that deception by job applicants is widespread, people do get caught. Indeed, nearly a quarter of the employers in the CIPD survey had dismissed employees because of it.

■ Absenteeism

If you've ever worked in a managerial role, you'll already know that absenteeism is a perennial headache for employers. The average worker now takes off about seven days every year, and the CBI puts the cost to British business of all those lost days at more than £12 billion.

Long-term absence is a more complex logistical problem, and an even bigger expense for organizations. The most common cause used to be back or muscular problems, but stress and other mental health concerns are catching up fast.

Employers are looking for fit, healthy people who will turn up for work every day. Making it clear that you take a responsible attitude towards your own health and fitness and rarely take time off should earn you points at job interviews.

■ Pet hates

All employers have their own particular dislikes when it comes to staff behaviour, but having talked to a large number of them over the years, we've drawn up a list (in no particular order) of the kind of characters who appear to bug them most.

- Poor attenders.
- Buck passers.
- People who don't listen.
- People who don't learn from their mistakes.
- People who disrupt their colleagues.
- People who are lazy.

Of course, your future boss may not be able to detect at the interview stage if you can't get out of bed in the morning, or are prone to blaming your colleagues for your own mistakes. So behaviour of that sort won't stop you *getting* a job. What it will do to your career prospects is another story.

■ Great people

When you're thinking about a change of career you will almost inevitably come across people (notably career professionals of one sort or another) who will tell you that particular job sectors are so competitive that you will find it virtually impossible to find work in them. Years of talking to employers suggests to us that this is not the case – and that's regardless of how many candidates are fighting for jobs in any particular sector, and regardless of the state of the economy. In our experience, shrewd employers are always looking for good people, and when they find them, they do their best to recruit them before someone else does.

■ Key points

- Employers are always on the lookout for good people.
- Many employers solve their recruitment problems by taking on the people who they believe have the most *potential*.
- Demand is highest for job candidates who are flexible and versatile.

Working for a small company might quickly allow you to become involved in almost everything the firm does. You could be in pole position for promotions and pay rises.

Chapter 8
Where do you want to work?

In this chapter you will find:

❏ Jobs serving the public

❏ Small businesses

❏ Big businesses

❏ The voluntary sector

Without even realizing it, you may have assumed automatically that your next workplace will be much the same as your last one. Yet it might just be that the very size or nature of your last place of employment was part of the reason you wanted to leave it.

The point here is that the size and business goals of the enterprise you work for could be of as much interest to you as the actual job you fancy doing. Too many people end up earning their living in surroundings they don't especially like. Not for nothing has the modern office been described as 'hell with fluorescent lighting'.

So, drawing on your experience so far, it's important to think about the size and working style of the company you are most likely to feel comfortable in. Some people who make a move from a small firm find that they love the buzz of a larger, ever-changing organization. Such places usually offer plenty of outside activities, and more opportunities to socialize with a wider range of people of your own age or interests.

Others who move from a large firm to a smaller one find it immediately rewarding to work in a smaller team – and often nearer to where they live.

Then there are those who actively prefer their own company to spending most of their time in an office with other people. You might not want to start your own business, but there are plenty of roles that involve frequent travelling, being outdoors, or working unsupervised for at least part of the week.

■ Jobs serving the public

Around one in five of all the jobs in Britain are in the public sector, which embraces teachers, doctors, nurses, the emergency services, postal workers, the armed forces, civil servants and local authority staff.

Until recently, the proportion of the UK workforce employed in the public sector had been gradually shrinking. In 1981 almost a third of us worked in the public sector. By 2001 this had shrunk to less than a fifth.

More recently, however, the government has been investing heavily in the public services – notably in the National Health Service and in education, the two areas that have seen the fastest growth. One benefit of this trend has been that the public sector has started to look more attractive to workers displaced by constant upheavals in the private sector. For example, some of those who lost their shirts when the high-tech bubble burst are finding that the teaching profession is now a more attractive job option.

As well as increasing public-service employment, the government has also been trying to improve the quality of public services. One of the features of this has been an attempt to lure high-quality potential workers with incentives such as training bursaries or small welcome bonuses for suitable recruits. This shortage of skilled and motivated people in the public-service sector could work to your advantage if you have the right qualifications and attitude.

As for pay, average starting salaries do tend to be a little lower than in the private sector, but are rising slightly more quickly, and such employment is often more secure.

■ Work with an attitude

People who work in the public services do tend to share a particular attitude or philosophy – a desire to improve provision in their chosen field. They often say that making a positive difference is an important reason for doing the work they do. Most firemen, nurses and police officers, for example, feel that they have a vocation and do a job that everyone recognizes as essential for the public good. A similar belief in the importance of public services is shared by thousands of people who work for local authorities, and by civil servants who toil behind the scenes to ensure that the laws or policies the government wants are workable in practice.

Public-service work often scores highly on the 'family-friendly' front, and flexible working arrangements are often available, depending on the role.

What's not so good about these kinds of jobs? Unsurprisingly, bureaucracy and paperwork came out top in a study by the government's own Audit Commission. Some things never seem to change.

■ Small can be beautiful

The vast majority of firms in Britain are small businesses, and many of those are really small: 95 per cent employ between one and 49 people. Next come what are often termed small-to-medium-sized enterprises (SMEs). There are around 27,000 of these in the UK, employing 50–249 people.

Small businesses are firms run by a few people who have to take on all the jobs required to keep the firm in profit. The enterprise will often be led personally by the founders or current owners, who will have the largest single financial stake in the business.

If you choose employment with a small company, you could well find yourself working in a limited physical space with a relatively small and un-changing group of people. It might be informal and friendly, but don't kid yourself that it'll be a breeze. The work may be as high-pressured as that with a large firm.

Unlike at a larger firm, though, your job interview might be quite casual. Small firms don't often have the resources to spend on training managers in state-of-the-art interviewing techniques. So if you go for a job in a small firm, the onus is more likely to be on you to make a good impression by asking lots of questions, rather than just sitting there and letting the interviewer do all the work.

■ Life on the small business front line

Working for a small company might quickly allow you to become involved in almost everything the firm does. If the company is going places, this means that you would not only build up great experience, but could also be in pole position for promotions and pay rises.

Something else worth bearing in mind is that increasing numbers of tiny technology and service companies have close relationships with much larger clients. During the course of your work, you would make contacts that could be invaluable when you start looking for a further job move. If you prove to be effective at your job, someone else might even approach you first.

But working for a tiny firm can have its drawbacks. Some small or family-owned companies exist only to provide a certain standard or style of living for their owners and their families. They are not all going places. Having gained further experience, you might have to move on yet again if you want a sub-stantial pay rise or to progress in your career.

Among the more common types of small business that employ gradu-ates are accountancy and law firms, high-technology companies and leisure companies. In the past, small business bosses used to complain that gradu-ates were too expensive to employ, lacked practical skills, didn't want to get their hands dirty and had unrealistic ambitions. Fortunately, that is changing.

All enterprises are having to become more professional to survive, and that means they need more talent.

So if you particularly rate variety, early responsibility and the chance to have your work noticed, a small firm is well worth considering. But equally, don't forget there are disadvantages to being a big fish in a small pond. If you perform badly, there may be nowhere to hide.

■ Why work for a small company?

Pros

- Chance of rapid involvement in many aspects of the business.
- You are likely to be given responsibility.
- Greater input into company procedures and future plans.
- See your ideas put into practice.
- You may have more say in your career development.
- Working as part of a small, dedicated team.
- Working hours may be more flexible.
- Less bureaucracy.

Cons

- Career path may be unclear.
- There may be no formal training – simply what you learn on the job.
- Need to work long hours as required to meet deadlines.
- Starting salaries often lower than at larger firms.
- Fewer benefits, such as a car, pension or health-club membership.

■ Big is beautiful – for some

Day-to-day life in a large firm can be very different from that in a small one. Big businesses tend to employ people to carry out specific tasks, and there is often little incentive (financial or otherwise) to do things outside your responsibilities. In large firms some workers may be less likely to feel that their contribution matters.

If you have your eye on working for a large firm, you might be surprised to discover that in 2002 there were only 7000 large businesses in the whole of the UK – that is, enterprises employing 250 people or more. Most base themselves in busy places with plenty of professional and skilled workers living within easy reach.

If you want to build a large-company career – say, in the media, pharmaceuticals, engineering or finance – it's important to start finding out more about the companies you want to target. For one thing, you will need to discover how and when they tend to recruit.

Competition is usually fierce in large firms. Your ability to progress would depend not only on your actual achievements, but also on getting the attention of senior managers on the lookout for those with the highest potential. But remember that senior managers come and go; it's not always easy to tell whose radar screen you need to be on. A good idea with large firms is to try to work out which areas of the business are regarded as 'core' – that is, those that are making money or are seen as promising areas for future growth. If you're in an area with limited business prospects, your personal promotion prospects may be zero however fantastic you are. Yes, business life is unfair sometimes.

■ Voluntary sector

There is also a fourth kind of organization that has recently become more prominent in the jobs market – Britain's voluntary or not-for-profit sector. This covers everything from welfare groups employing a single paid manager to housing associations, trade unions and national charities, such as the NSPCC, Shelter, Oxfam and Amnesty. As things stand, there are over 180,000 registered charities in the UK.

This is now a big sector of the job market, with over half a million paid employees – that is more workers than are employed in the City of London, in farming, or in the car industry. One in 50 of all full-time employees in the UK now has a paid job in the voluntary sector. They work alongside 3 million more part-time and unpaid staff.

Among other things, voluntary organizations are defined as: independent of government and business; bodies that do not distribute profits to shareholders; groups that provide benefits to others as well as their own members.

The voluntary sector remains a favourite choice for people leaving the armed services or wanting a career change. It certainly offers a bewildering array of roles and ways of working, with much to offer those transferring their skills from other fields. But strong efforts are being made to attract a new, younger generation of workers. The largest charities have jobs that are comparable with many found in the private sector – from accountants, marketing specialists and public relations officers to social workers, campaigners, lawyers and scientific advisers.

These are roles where you need to consider carefully the kind of organization you will be joining. The work may be paid, but you will need to be in sympathy with the aims and objectives of the charity or welfare group you hope to join. One of the best ways of demonstrating this is to build up volunteering experience.

If you are interested in further exploring what 'organizational culture' might suit you, the test on the US website **www.careerleader.com/sstn/culture-test. html** may be of interest.

Voluntary work may not be the sector to choose if top pay is your priority (although some jobs within it *are* highly paid). Yet, interestingly, surveys have repeatedly found that not-for-profit workers are generally happier and more fulfilled than those in other professions.

■ A word about bosses

It's sometimes said that people rarely leave a post because they can't stand the job. Repeated surveys have shown that by far the most common reason why people leave their jobs is because they can't stand the boss.

How your boss operates can make your working life a pleasure or a pain. A good leader creates a positive working environment and can raise your game on a bad day. Over time, a poor one can make you feel incompetent and lower your self-esteem.

Being able to get on well with your boss is possibly even more essential in a tiny organization. Some small-business bosses are prone to 'micromanage' – getting involved in everything their employees do – which can be frustrating if you'd rather be left alone.

Don't wait for a formal interview to size up your potential employer. If you have a particular job in mind, see if you can get to speak to the boss informally first. If you have contacts, ask around.

■ So what makes a great place to work?

There can be no simple answer to this one. It depends so much on your own priorities and on what stage you are at in your career.

You might prefer a fast-moving organization, where managers set goals and leave you to deliver them with the minimum of direct supervision. Equally, you might prefer stability and for your work tasks to be more clearly directed.

Most of all, a good workplace is one that motivates you personally. You will find it easier to assess a potential employer if you refer back to the personal drivers you selected in Chapter 5.

Below you will find some features of organizations that employees often value or look for. It's unlikely that any one firm would offer all of them, but they are some of the tangible benefits that organizations may offer to keep their people happy and motivated.

- **Flexible employment** – willingness to tailor contracts to suit your personal or family needs, including part-time working, flexible working hours, allowing unpaid leave or sabbaticals.
- **Benefit options** – ability for employees to select from a range of fringe benefits. These might include profit share or share option schemes, private health insurance, car provision or loans, training and help with tuition, enhanced or tailored pension arrangements, and disability benefits.
- **Personal development** – commitment to develop staff through formal training, coaching and continuing support. This might include regular career discussions, and learning or shadowing more demanding tasks in other departments to widen your experience and develop your talents.
- **Health and social facilities** – anything from organized social events to exercise classes, sports and social club membership, from in-house therapists and personal trainers to cafeterias with healthy menus.
- **Mentoring** – organizational commitment to providing experienced mentors (guides) to help less experienced staff reflect on their progress and goals.
- **Work–life balance** – formal commitment to supporting workers so that they can meet their obligations to young children, partners or elderly relatives.

■ What's your ideal working environment?

Thinking about your ideal working surroundings can guide you towards possible careers – or at least steer you away from the kinds of environment you know you wouldn't enjoy. So this is a good time to reflect on the different organizations described in this chapter. Here are some questions you might like to consider.

■ Are you based mainly in the UK, or do you travel extensively or work abroad?

■ Are you usually in an office, on the road, based at home, or do you spend most of your time outdoors?

■ Do you work for a large multinational company, a medium-sized firm, a small business, or are you self-employed?

■ Can you see yourself working in the public sector, for a voluntary organization or charity, or only for a commercial firm?

■ Are you doing shift work, normal office hours or working part-time or flexible hours?

■ Do you work with a large group of people, an ever-changing group, a small team, or do you spend much of your time alone?

■ What kinds of people do you work with? (For example, are they like you, or do you have dealings with people of different ages or outlooks?)

■ Key points

■ The size and goals of the enterprise you work for could be of as much interest to you as the actual field you fancy working in.

■ Most people working in the public sector have a desire to improve people's lives in some way. Pay may be a little lower, but jobs may be slightly more secure.

■ Small firms are becoming more dynamic and can offer rapid promotion and hands-on experience.

■ Large companies are still a top choice for those wanting to build a professional career with established paths to promotion.

■ Thinking ahead and imagining your preferred working conditions and the roles you might like to carry out will greatly aid your career search.

The best plan is to widen your search, so as to explore the greatest possible range of opportunities.

Chapter 9
What sort of job do you want?

In this chapter you will find:

❏ Life goals

❏ Your wish list

❏ Career research

❏ Your job specification

Like all important life decisions, career moves need careful thought. We all think we know that, but many people often pick their next job after far less research than they'd devote to choosing a holiday or buying a car.

If you liked your old job but it came to an end, you may well be looking for a new one that's just like it. The reality is that you probably won't be able to find another exactly like your last one, so you can save yourself a lot of effort by not wasting energy looking for an identikit job. Others may be daunted because they feel they have to find that one 'perfect' job waiting out there with their name on it. In both cases, the best plan is not to narrow things down, but to do the complete opposite – widen your search so as to explore the greatest possible range of opportunities.

If you have already worked through the previous chapters, you should have thought a lot more about what you want. Now it's time to start applying what you have learnt about yourself to search for the kind of work that suits you down to the ground.

■ Test your job ideas against your life goals

How can you make better job choices? The entrepreneur Emma Harrison is the founder of A4e, a national employment and training agency. She was a mentor on the Channel 4 TV business show *Make Me a Million*.

Emma suggests finding a quiet moment, getting a pencil and piece of paper and noting down what you really want in life. Imagine taking all the things you most want off a shelf and putting them into a basket. You might include happiness, good health, a fancy car or motorbike, a business of your own, a house, a new circle of friends, lovely holidays – whatever you want. Then you can start thinking about what work to do next or what ideas you can develop.

Referring back to your list is important because, according to Emma Harrison, you should take a job only if it helps get you nearer to one or other of your stated goals. For example, if you put 'happiness' as a goal, and you know in your heart of hearts that the job you are looking at is much the same as your last one, it will almost certainly make you miserable. The first job you come across may not always be the right one. And that's free advice from someone whose businesses have been valued at some £50 million!

So one of the first things you need to do is symbolically take off the job description badge that tells the world you are a sales executive, an administrator, an engineer, or whatever you are. Far better to replace it with one that describes what you are capable of.

START DRAWING UP YOUR WISHLIST

Bearing in mind your experience and what you have learnt about yourself so far, see if you can start to work out:

- The business sector or general area you think you'd enjoy working in.
- Where you might like to work – near to home, in another town, overseas?
- The kind of co-workers you'd choose to work with – young crowd, small team, experienced professionals, on your own as much as possible?
- How your ideal job would enhance or at least complement your lifestyle.

■ Think broad areas, not specific roles

Remember that employers want to take on only flexible people who can help make their firm more successful and profitable (see Chapter 7). This means that if, for example, you are set on working in fashion design, you should research the many other possibilities in the wider field of, say, product design and consultancy. Could you imagine yourself designing home textiles, or advising a client on new uniforms for their workforce?

Let's suppose your job at a local engineering concern is coming to an end. A little research could lead you to discover that modern engineering offers suitable candidates a wide array of opportunities at home and overseas. Once you find out more about these, you will be better able to judge whether what is on offer locally is still your best bet.

IMAGINE WHAT YOU MIGHT BE GOOD AT

You might feel that no one knows you better than you do yourself, but that's not always true. It's sometimes easier to spot other people's unique qualities than it is to pin down our own. So here is an exercise you can do with a friend – ideally, someone else who is also thinking about a career change.

Sit down, each with a pad and pen, and start listing every single quality you think best describes the other person. Put down as many as you can. Here are some suggestions to get you going.

Qualities

Able	Fast	Precise
Agile	Flexible	Resourceful
Assertive	Forthright	Responsible
Careful	Friendly	Selfless
Caring	Hard working	Sensitive
Communicative	Helpful	Sharp-eyed
Conscientious	Honest	Steady-handed
Creative	Humorous	Strong
Dedicated	Imaginative	Supportive
Determined	Insightful	Thorough
Discreet	Intuitive	Trustworthy
Easygoing	Nimble	Understanding
Energetic	Organized	Unsentimental
Ethical	Perceptive	Willing

When you have both finished, swap lists so that you can see what's been written about you. Now add anything else you think is true of you to the list – things your friend didn't think of.

When you've each done that, look through the following list and note down any categories that interest you, or that you think might interest you in the future. Again, don't just rely on what's listed here – see if you or your friend can think of anything else to add.

Interests and skills

Architecture	Computers and IT	Designing
Art	Cookery and food	Driving
Astronomy	Countryside	Entertaining
Beauty	Craft	Fashion
Books	Creative writing	Film
Building	Crime	Finance
Camping	Current affairs	Fixing things
Carpentry	Dance	Gardens
Cars	Danger	Geography
Collecting	Decorating	Hair

Health	Organizing events	Sport
History	Outdoor activities	Theatre
Keeping records	Performing	Travel
Languages	Sailing and the sea	TV
Maths	Science	Walking
Meeting new people	Selling	Wildlife
Music		

Now you should have two lists each. Next have a look at the final list below. It shows various sectors or fields of business activity where people are employed.

Job sectors

Animals	Hotels and catering	Retail
Aerospace	Internet/IT/computers	Sales
Banking and finance	Law	Social services
Building	Manufacturing	Teaching
Engineering	Media	Telecoms
Food	Nature	Tourism and leisure
Government	Police and security	Transport
Hospitals and health		

Working down your first two lists of personal characteristics and interests, see if you can imagine a match between any of these and your list of job sectors. For example, if you have 'caring' in your first list, you might imagine yourself working in animal welfare, doing something in a hospital, managing a fitness centre, being a countryside warden, working with children in a hostel, perhaps doing specialist teaching, or starting a business involving looking after people such as a hotel or bed and breakfast. So you'd tick animals, hospitals, hotels, nature, social services, teaching or tourism. If you have, say, 'designing' in your second list, you might tick aerospace, engineering, internet, manufacturing, media or retail. Each area or sector encompasses hundreds of different potential jobs you could explore.

■ It's all on file

Once you've short-listed some potential sectors, it's time to get stuck into more detailed career research. Today, thanks to the internet, there's a wealth of information about working in business, industry and the public services that you can browse online at the touch of a mouse. If you come across a likely-looking organization, go to its website to find out more. If you can't use a personal computer to look up websites, now's the time to learn as a matter of priority: local libraries are a good starting point.

Try to discover more about a range of firms operating in the industry, trade, profession or service in which you are interested, and the variety of roles within them. You can read things such as annual reports and press releases, or even watch corporate movies or presentations. Large employers tend to give out detailed information about how they work, when they recruit and the kind of candidates they are looking for.

Professional and industrial bodies also publish lots of useful information you can print out or download. Almost all provide links you can follow to member companies or other representative bodies that may be able to help you.

■ Exploring what jobs exist

A great way of finding out about all sorts of jobs is by taking a look at the Jobs4U Careers Database found at **www.connexions-direct.com**. Connexions is officially aimed at those aged 13–19, but here you will find a comprehensive guide to careers, from AA patrol person to zoologist. There's information on everything from the work environment, entry requirements and skills required to pay, conditions and related occupations.

Unfortunately, there is no adult counterpart to Connexions. Instead there is NextStep (**www.nextstep.org.uk**), an integrated advice service that provides local training information. The network gives priority to adults who have yet to achieve five GCSEs at grade C or equivalent.

Scotland and Wales (unlike England) provide statutory, free careers guidance for all adults, and both have useful websites: **www.careers-scotland. org.uk** and **www.careers-wales.com**.

Other useful websites for job-hunting include:

www.jobcentreplus.gov.uk has a jobs database, and the 'Worktrain' section allows you to search for jobs, as well as finding out about training and careers.

www.prospects.ac.uk is a leading graduate careers website, with suggestions for careers and links to UK university careers services.

www.careers.lon.ac.uk/output/Page65.asp contains lots of advice and help on career choice and job-hunting.

www.doctorjob.co.uk has graduate recruitment information, careers advice and jobs.

www.fish4.co.uk/iad/jobs is a commercial site with useful information on careers in secretarial, sales, marketing, IT, engineering, construction and accounting.

Depending on where you live, numerous other local authority, educational and enterprise organizations may provide career services. Your local library or Citizens Advice Bureau is the place to track them down.

■ Map out your own world of work

If you want more job ideas, another good place to look is the comprehensive website **www.learndirect-futures.co.uk**, which is funded by the government's Learning and Skills Council. This carries essential information on over 700 different jobs, including the nature of the work itself, the hours, pay and training requirements. Once you have registered, look for the questionnaires that take you through a simple process to arrive at your personalized World of Work map. This identifies a selection of jobs that are the best matches with your stated interests and skills.

If you enjoy getting ideas in this way, there's a more comprehensive American site that matches careers to personal interests: **http://online. onecenter.org**.

Click on Career Change within **www.vault.com** and you will find a useful section – 'A day in the life of a…' – where you can get a taster of what the jobs you might be considering are actually like.

■ Information is power

Hard information about the minimum qualification and training requirements can sometimes bring your job ambitions down to earth with a bump. For example, if you fancy becoming an airline pilot but fail to get yourself spon-sored by an airline, you will find that your training could cost you a whopping £50,000.

On the positive side, you may also discover there are more ways into your field of interest than you may have realized. Suppose civil engineering appeals to you: a quick search would reveal that there are at least four recog-nized ways into the profession, ranging from studying for a degree to a voca-tional route requiring less exacting entry qualifications than university.

Or perhaps you are thinking about becoming a pharmacist. In this case entry is by a degree offered at 16 universities. You would need a minimum of five good GCSEs and three science A levels, including chemistry. You would discover that although two-thirds of pharmacists work in shops, others have roles in hospitals, industry and research and development. You might also be inspired to explore related careers you might not even have thought of – bio-medical science, anyone?

It's important to remember that competition for places in some fields is such that, in practice, you would need more than the minimum stated qualifi-cations to stand a chance of beating other applicants.

■ Comparing jobs and what to look for

Research widely in each of the sectors you find appealing. Don't try to rush this process – it will be time well spent. Try to compare the merits of each, and think about the following things:

■ What the actual job would involve each day.
■ The kind of people who do the job and the skills they use to do it.
■ The range of companies or organizations in the field.
■ The entry requirements and training you would need.

Bear your longer-term goals in mind too. How does work with a particular firm or in a specific industry stack up? Does it:

■ Match your skills, interests and preferred subject choices?
■ Allow you to use or continue studying the subjects you enjoy?
■ Offer you the kind of work environment you would thrive in?
■ Have the potential to deliver the income and lifestyle you would like?

■ Read the newspaper backwards

The business and specialist sections of daily and regional newspapers are mines of useful information and can give you a feel for the state of entire industries. You may be surprised at how out of touch you have become while focusing on doing one particular job. For example, take the transfer of many call centre jobs from the UK to Asia. Stories connected to these events were all faithfully documented in the business pages way before they reached wider national attention.

When you are job-hunting, discovering that a company is suffering from falling profits should set the alarm bells ringing: you might face budget cuts, recruitment freezes or takeovers.

Trade sites for particular industries can also provide an early insight into who is hiring and firing. For example, www.computing.co.uk is a widely used and fast-changing source of news, information and jobs being advertised in the IT industry, while www.inpharm.com is practically a one-stop directory for senior staff in the pharmaceutical and healthcare sector.

■ Turn your interests and skills into a career

Most people know of someone who has managed to turn a childhood hobby or talent into a full-time job – for example, a toy car enthusiast who became a garage owner, or perhaps a bookworm or music collector who managed to start a thriving local business.

What about drawing on your enthusiasm for, say, travel, transport, animals, gardening or the countryside? If you have practical skills, could you turn hobbies such as doing people's hair or sorting out problems with computers into some kind of business (see Chapter 10)? Anything you feel strongly about might offer scope for devising a career plan.

Have a good think too about your personal opinions and ideas. For example, you might have particular views about the treatment of children, health, the environment, or the workings of government. If you do, put that passion to good use. Spend a little time investigating work in areas where someone like you could actually make a difference – for example, in the law, social services, conservation or some aspect of government.

DRAW UP YOUR OWN JOB SPECIFICATION

Think broadly about your present and future skills, learning and employment preferences, and add any conclusions you arrive at to your list.

My skills

■ Do you like the idea of drawing on professional skills that took you several years to learn, or do you prefer the idea of gaining your skills while being employed?

■ Do you rely on using negotiation or persuasion skills to succeed in your job or get on with your colleagues?

■ Do you like the idea of using technical or mechanical skills at work?

■ Is being able to give free rein to your creative skills important to you?

The skills I'd like to use at work:

_____

_____

_____

My level at work

■ How senior do you want to become within your organization?

■ Does being responsible for the supervision of others appeal to you?

■ Do you see yourself as a middle manager or a director?

■ Will you be content to reach a certain level of responsibility or always be striving for promotion?

My ideal level would be:

_____

_____

_____

My role at work

- Do you see yourself managing others or carrying out a specialist role?
- Do you play a supportive role, anticipating the needs of team members?
- Do you enjoy working to deadlines?
- Are you designing or creating new products or services?
- Can you find new customers and sell them products or services?
- Does your ideal role involve measuring, analysing or providing information?
- Would you be happy to repeat tasks every day, week, month or quarter?
- Would you like to be involved in teaching, guiding or motivating others?
- Would you like to talk to people in large groups?
- Do you have an overriding concern to help others?

My ideal role would involve:

_____

_____

_____

▦ Key points

- Don't act on impulse. Instead, do your research thoroughly. See if you can pick out broad employment sectors in which you might enjoy working.
- Use resources to find out more about the range of jobs in each sector. What does the work involve day to day?
- Taking each role that interests you, what further study or training would you need and what are the minimum entry requirements?
- Talk to as many people who are in work as possible.
- Visit as many different kinds of workplace as you can.
- Think realistically about your ideal role at work. What skills do you use and how high do you expect to climb?

You will need to work out exactly what it is you think you can sell, who your customers will be, and how much you will need to charge to make a profit.

Chapter 10
Going it alone

In this chapter you will find:

❏ Running your own show

❏ Market research

❏ Finance

❏ Tax

❏ Insurance

❏ Are you an entrepreneur?

If you've recently been made redundant or are leaving your present job, the idea of becoming self-employed or starting a business of your own may seem immediately appealing. But then again, it's probably going to be a lot of hassle. Why risk setting up on your own when so many new small businesses fail? How about making yourself a cup of tea, giving up on your silly dreams and finding another salaried job instead?

According to serial entrepreneur and Princes Trust business mentor Martin Webb, those are just the kind of comments you may be subjected to by family, friends and former workmates. If you don't allow yourself to be put off, you could be on your way to passing your first hurdle.

Having said that, it's important to listen carefully to all the advice that comes your way – even the unhelpful stuff – as you might get some great ideas that will improve your chances of making a go of it.

■ Running your own show

As politicians never tire of telling us, small businesses are the lifeblood of a successful economy. Everyone from the chancellor of the exchequer downwards is trying to promote an 'enterprise culture'. Britain now has well over 3 million owner-managed businesses.

The number one benefit of becoming self-employed is that you are a free agent, released from the tyranny of office politics and the whims of your employer. But – and it's a big but – you will no longer be able to count on a weekly or monthly income. You may be running your own show, but you will still have to answer the phone, deal with suppliers and clients, pay all the bills, open the post, deal with paperwork and the taxman – and change the ink cartridge in the printer. You may have the freedom to break off to collect the children from school, but you may find yourself stressed out and working punishing hours. You would also need to make your own provisions for sick pay and a retirement pension. For a long while too you can probably kiss goodbye to lazy weekends and expensive treats.

■ What kind of business shall I start?

If you have no idea what you actually want to do, the best plan is to start with your existing skills (see Chapter 6). What talents do you have that you might be able to market or develop to generate an income? Perhaps you already have some hobby, interest, craft or part-time work experience that you might be able to transform into a nice little earner. It could be that you are already known for being an ace repairer of bikes or computers. Maybe you have a reputation as a bit of a business troubleshooter, or have already been asked if you are ever available to do freelance work.

You might be able to spot a gap in the services on offer down your local high street, or perhaps on an industrial estate or in a nearby town. It's also worth considering the things you are passionate about. For example, if you are a serious foodie, you options could include catering for local events, opening a delicatessen or café, making and selling your own produce, supplying restaurants and shops, or dipping a toe into retail by setting up your own market stall.

It's important to think laterally. Some of the best enterprises seem to emerge when people draw on expertise or knowledge they have built up in one field and apply it to a more specialist area or niche. For example, Chrissie Rucker worked on a women's magazine before establishing the White Company in her loft. She specializes in selling the kind of bedlinen and luxury household items she loves but had difficulty finding in the shops. Initially, she did all her business online, but is now opening stores around the country.

Software engineer Nigel Biggs felt there was little challenge in his job working for a giant computer corporation. He left, managed to find some contract work and developed a particular interest in what was then the relatively new field of digital imaging. He went on to found Pixology, now a European leader in digital imaging software.

■ Take time to do your homework

Whatever you think you might do next, you won't get far unless you do lots of homework. Don't be surprised if it takes a year to work up your ideas and test them out. The last thing you want to do is to sacrifice your income from a paid job until you are ready to take the plunge. Keep on good terms with your previous employer if you can. You may well need him or her to write you a reference – and your old firm might even put some work your way. You could persuade them to let you work part time while you prepare to go solo.

■ Research the market

You will need to do a thorough investigation of your potential market, working out exactly what it is you think you can sell, who your customers will be and how much you will need to charge to make a profit. Can you identify your main competitors? Is there anything you could do to give your product or service an edge over that already offered by your rivals?

Try not to be tempted to offer too wide a range of products or services. And there's no escaping the need to prepare a realistic and convincing business plan, an essential document going over your projected finances.

■ In the footsteps of giants

Turning a mere idea into profitable reality requires a combination of knowledge, imagination, nerve and dogged determination. Don't get too hung up about whether you have the temperament to be the next Martha Lane-Fox or Sir Alan Sugar. Being competent, organized and able to deliver your service cost-effectively will get you a long way, but you will need staying power. It's a sad fact that a third of new businesses fail within five years of being started. Research suggests that many of these had financial problems from the very start.

Fortunately, there are plenty of success stories to inspire you: just keep an eye on the many regular small business features in most daily newspapers, or the enterprise section of any large bookshop.

Take the founder of the Virgin empire, Sir Richard Branson. He started his business career at the age of nine – with a venture growing Christmas trees. Unfortunately, rabbits ate them. Undeterred, he later moved into student publishing, before graduating to the music and airline business. He'd be the first to admit that he's had plenty of failures along with the successes.

One of the world's most successful entrepreneurs is the American Warren Buffett with his investment company Berkshire Hathaway. He began in business buying multipacks of soft drinks, splitting them up and selling the individual cans to friends. Now, some 60 years on, he still puts money only into products he understands personally – such as Coca-Cola. It really is worth sticking to what you know.

■ How will you trade?

Many enterprises are not formally constituted as companies: they operate as individuals working for themselves. But you will need to establish a clear legal entity for your business, which should take one of three defined forms:

- **Sole trader** – the quickest, simplest and easiest kind of enterprise to set up, but you are solely responsible for any debts.
- **Partnership** – similar to a sole trader except that two or more people run the enterprise and share the risks and rewards.
- **Limited company** – an entity that is legally separate from the individuals who own or run it. Such firms must be registered at Companies House and have 'limited liability'. This means the owners have some personal financial protection if the company should fail. Limited companies are more complicated to set up.
- **Cooperative** – this is a business that is collectively owned and controlled by two or more workers. (It differs from a partnership in terms of liability and taxation.)
- **Franchise** – this is an agreement allowing an individual the right to run a local branch of a business that someone else has set up, for example, BodyShop.

■ Keep proper records

Your venture will almost certainly end in disaster if you fail to keep accurate and thorough records from the start. You may feel you cannot afford help with keeping your books. Fortunately, there's now a wide range of off-the-peg computer software that will help with much of the donkey work, such as sorting out your VAT returns. However, you may want to seek some basic finance or management training before you begin trading.

■ A word about finance

As someone who is self-employed, you will need money to live on, as well as start-up finance to get your business going – probably far more than you might have expected. It's crucial to think about where the money to establish your new business will come from. You can't afford not to plan every aspect of your finances thoroughly. According to the business credit specialists

Dun & Bradstreet, nine out of ten small business failures are due to insufficient funding, poor management and lack of planning.

You may be able to get money from various sources, including:

- Family or friends.
- Grants from charities or trusts.
- Loans from banks and financial institutions.
- Investment by 'angels' or venture capitalists (in exchange for a share in your business or a slice of your profits – or both).

■ Tax can be taxing

If you become self-employed, you need to register with Revenue & Customs. The tax system works differently when you are not an employee. There are special allowances and concessions you can claim, but you are responsible for paying tax on what you earn. You will need to set aside enough money to meet the inevitable tax demands once you are up and running. Most people find that they need the help of an accountant. Depending on the turnover of your business, you may also need to register for VAT.

■ Where will you trade from?

Working from home is likely to be the cheapest option, but you will need to ensure your mortgage or tenancy agreement does not prevent you from doing this. Depending on the nature of your business, you may need planning consent from your local council.

If you decide to trade from bought or rented premises, you should consider how much space you will need and what that will cost you in rent.

You will also need to take the cost of heating, lighting and ventilation into account. You must check the property is approved for business use. Again, planning permission may be needed. If you are considering buying or renting premises, you should see a solicitor or chartered surveyor.

Some people start out trading from a market stall. Your local authority will have details of locations and charges.

An increasingly popular option is to test the market by selling goods online using auction sites, notably eBay. This and other websites also host virtual stores where you can offer goods or services without needing to set up complicated and secure transaction systems yourself.

■ Other costs of doing business

Whether you are working from a shop, from your own factory, office or warehouse, you will need to pay business rates. Changes have recently been introduced, including a new rate relief scheme to help the smallest businesses that trade from one property in England. A few kinds of business premises are exempt, notably those on agricultural land.

As a self-employed person, you may have to pay national insurance contributions for yourself and any employees – it all depends on how much you or they earn. The payment of contributions will affect the benefits that you can claim in the future.

You may also have to spend money ensuring that your workplace meets health and safety requirements. Further information on what's required is available from your local health and safety executive or the environmental health department of your council.

■ It's essential to insure

Some kinds of business insurance are optional, but there are some you are required to take out by law. These are:

- **Employer's liability insurance** – essential if you employ other people. It provides cover for any claims made by employees who are injured or get sick as a result of their employment.
- **Vehicle insurance** – vehicles used for business purposes have to be insured, even if there is already a policy in operation for private use.
- **Public liability insurance** – this covers you against any claims by people who have been injured or had property damaged as a result of carelessness by you or your employees.
- **Premises insurance** – home policies cover only claims arising from residential use.
- **Contents, stock and materials insurance** – this is to cover the replacement costs of damaged or stolen stock, materials and the contents of the premises.
- **Health and accident insurances** – these pay out a regular income or lump sum if you cannot work because of an accident or sickness.

■ Employing other people

If you provide work for others, you will be responsible for paying wages, tax, National Insurance contributions and Working Tax Credit where relevant. You will have to meet the requirements of employment law and health and safety regulations.

■ Getting further advice

Most high street banks have sections that specialize in helping small businesses, and most produce free leaflets. The Citizens Advice Bureau, chambers of commerce, the Business Links, Learning and Skills Councils and local business advice organizations are also ready to help, usually for free.

The web is a rich source of advice for wannabe entrepreneurs. As always, Google or another good search engine is your oyster. Beware sites that charge you for services until you are sure what you are getting. The following are all good sites for starters:

www.starttalkingideas.org
www.businesslink.gov.uk
www.princes-trust.org.uk
www.shell-livewire.org

■ The entrepreneurial gene

Anyone can mug up on the necessary components of a profitable business. But you still need to have the right spark to create one yourself – the 'entrepreneurial gene', as some people call it. Successful business owners are resourceful and energetic: they have a need to succeed. They like to solve problems. They have the ability to make confident decisions and to persuade and motivate others. They are also versatile – business owners need to wear lots of different hats. So do you think you have an entrepreneur's head on you? Why not try our quiz to help you find out?

DO YOU HAVE WHAT IT TAKES TO BE AN ENTREPRENEUR?

No questionnaire like this can genuinely reveal if you're cut out to be your own boss and well on your way to making your first million. But you can at least find out if you share some of the traits typical of a serial entrepreneur.

Circle 'YES' or 'NO' to the following questions, and remember – there are no right or wrong answers, but be honest!

1. Do you start each day feeling positive?   YES/NO
2. When things go wrong, do you pick yourself up quickly   YES/NO
   and try again?
3. Do you like yourself and who you are?   YES/NO
4. Do you like to make things happen instead of waiting for   YES/NO
   them to happen?
5. Do you get discouraged easily if things don't go to plan?   YES/NO
6. If you did something differently from others, would you   YES/NO
   worry about what they might think?
7. Are you a good salesperson? Can you sell your ideas to   YES/NO
   others?
8. Can you get on with people you don't like?   YES/NO
9. Are you a good judge of character – could you hire   YES/NO
   (and fire) the right people if you wanted to expand your
   business?
10. Does pressure feed you rather than get to you?   YES/NO
11. Do you observe what is happening around you, and have   YES/NO
    a sixth sense for what people want?
12. Do you usually learn from your mistakes?   YES/NO
13. Are you a good organizer?   YES/NO
14. Are you looking for better ways to do things – for example,   YES/NO
    while doing this test, were you thinking of ways to make
    it better?
15. As a child, were you always finding ways of making money?   YES/NO
16. Do you have family or friends who could help you get   YES/NO
    started, ideally who have small-business experience?
17. Do you have the ability to think through possible outcomes   YES/NO
    and take steps to ensure that they do, or don't, happen?
18. Can you make quick decisions and feel comfortable about   YES/NO
    them afterwards?
19. Do you relate well to people of different backgrounds?   YES/NO
20. Can you start a conversation if you find yourself in a room   YES/NO
    full of strangers?
21. Are you comfortable talking to groups of people?   YES/NO
22. Do you keep to deadlines you have been set?   YES/NO

23. When you start something, do you see it through rather YES/NO than get sidetracked?

24. Can you manage to juggle several projects at the same YES/NO time?

25. In a discussion, can you persuade people to change their YES/NO mind by the force of your arguments?

26. Can you express yourself well so that people are interested YES/NO in what you are talking about?

27. Are you happy about being always on the lookout for YES/NO work?

28. Do you know the difference between gross and net profits? YES/NO

29. Do you understand terms such as assets, liabilities, goodwill YES/NO and working capital, or are you interested in finding out?

30. Would you be happy to telephone strangers or knock at YES/NO their doors and try to sell them things?

31. Are you willing to work long hours and go without holi- YES/NO days?

32. If you have any savings, would you be willing to invest and YES/NO possibly lose a large proportion of them?

33. Would you be prepared to accept a lower standard of YES/NO living until your business became profitable?

34. Are you prepared to clean the toilets, empty the waste YES/NO bins and unjam the photocopier?

35. Do you feel a need to achieve something on your own? YES/NO

36. Are you sometimes uncomfortable with authority? YES/NO

37. Do people sometimes think you are a bit of a chancer? YES/NO

38. Do you tend to have stronger opinions than your friends? YES/NO

39. Can you easily discard or change your plans when circum- YES/NO stances dictate?

40. Unless you can control your own work, do you get bored? YES/NO

What's your score?

Give yourself one point for every 'YES' you circled.

■ **If you scored over 30 points:** On the face of it you have many of the characteristics of a self-made business person. You like to look at possibilities, make your own decisions and change direction as necessary to achieve your goals.

- **If you scored 20–30 points:** You have some, but not all, of the qualities of a successful entrepreneur. Have a look at what follows this quiz to see if you can spot any of your potential weaknesses. If you're still keen to be the next Sir Richard Branson, you could start trying to make up for any deficiencies by seeking out the appropriate training. Comfort yourself with the thought that once your new business is doing well, you can hire people with the skills or patience you think you lack.
- **If you scored under 20 points:** Being an entrepreneur may not be for you. Running your own business involves lots of hassle, so maybe you'd be happier in a more secure job, working for someone else who can take the risks.

■ Entrepreneurs are a special breed

Over the years there have been lots of studies made about people who run their own businesses. One interesting finding was that such people often have strong opinions – and not just about their own work. Football, religion, economics, local issues… it doesn't really matter what – everything seems to provoke a powerful response. If you are going to risk your time and money in your own venture, you must have a strong conviction that it is going to succeed.

Sometimes it helps to team up with someone who has a different outlook on life. Brent Hoberman, the co-founder of Lastminute.com, the online travel and entertainment website, was always totally convinced that an internet company selling unsold plane and theatre tickets would make a fantastic business. His partner in the project, Martha Lane-Fox, was less sure about the idea, but gave it her best shot. The combination of unbridled enthusiasm and practicality worked brilliantly. Together they grew the business and were soon taking it public on the stock market – only to see the dot.com bubble burst and the value of their shares plunge to almost nothing. Yet they kept their nerve and were able to overcome huge setbacks to rebuild the business, which they subsequently sold for £577 million.

Entrepreneurs often seem to be the kind of people who resent being told what to do. They like to be the boss, not work for one. Some even have a history of getting into trouble at home or at school. They also appear to have a strong need for achievement, which translates as great self-motivation. A good decision for an entrepreneur would probably be a gamble or a risk for the rest of us. People who run their own business often fail to see the pitfalls that others see straight away. On the positive side, this means they sometimes achieve the apparently impossible. But they also rush in where angels fear to tread. So if you answered yes to most of the questions in the quiz, and you are definitely up for starting a business, you will need to be ready to stick with it if the going gets rough.

■ What makes a great entrepreneur?

Among the qualities you will need are:

- **Drive** – demonstrated by your self-motivation, vigour, initiative, good health, persistence and the ability to take responsibility for your actions.
- **Thinking ability** – that's original, creative, critical and analytical thinking.
- **People skills** – you will have to be sociable, considerate, cheerful, tactful and emotionally stable.
- **Communication skills** – writing, speaking, comprehending and responding appropriately to your customers.
- **Technical knowledge** – able to manage the actual manufacture or delivery of goods and services.

■ Checklist for aspiring entrepreneurs

It's always a good idea to study why and how others have failed in business so that you don't make the same mistakes. Such experiences can teach us a great deal. Duncan Cheatle, who runs networking events for entrepreneurs (**www.supper-club.net**) has come up with these top ten tips for people who want to run their own business.

1. **Do it for passion, not money.** Things don't happen overnight, so do something you feel passionate about. Do not start something with an exit and a fortune in mind: you'll probably fail. This was commonplace during the dot.com era, when people came up with ludicrous business ideas.

2. **Do something you know about.** Philip Green, the retail entrepreneur, says that he and his family invest only in retail businesses because that's what they understand. If you go into something you know little or nothing about, you will soon be out of your depth.

3. **Don't give up too soon.** Successful businesses are usually very different from those described in their original business plan. Try something, and if it isn't working, try it a different way.

4. **Have a mentor.** First-time entrepreneurs often fail because they don't have someone experienced they can turn to for advice as things crop up. Everyone needs a sounding board.

5. **Get the funding right.** Businesses often spend too much time chasing the wrong form of funding from the wrong people. It can take a long time to get people to pay you.

6. **Manage your money well.** Ensure you have financial plans and see if you are keeping to them.

7. **Build sales before anything else.** A lot of people spend too much time perfecting the design of their stationery or website instead of getting out there and making sales.

8. **Don't try to rush.** Winning customers takes time, so sell, tweak what you are offering, then sell again.

9. **Be wary of advice.** Friends may mean well, but they can lead you astray.

10. **Keep things flexible.** You don't want to get locked into anything you can't get out of easily – such as taking on more staff.

■ Key points

■ Look for entrepreneurial leanings in your past and current activities, and discover if you're really cut out to go it alone.

■ Do as much background reading and research as you can. There are lots of success stories to inspire you and to learn from.

■ Always build up expertise in your chosen field before preparing a proper business plan and taking the plunge.

Always check with potential employers that the qualification you have in mind is actually the right one for the job you want.

Chapter 11
Updating your skills

In this chapter you will find:

❑ Workplace training

❑ Types of study

❑ Where to start

❑ Funding

If you're wondering whether now is a good time to update your skills or qualifications, the answer is yes because it's *always* a good time.

High-calibre job applicants are in short supply – employers in every sector complain that they don't see anywhere near enough people with the skills they need. In fact, according to a study by the Chartered Institute of Personnel and Development (CIPD), a lack of specialist skills is the most common reason why employers struggle to fill job vacancies. So provided you carefully match the training you do to the requirements of the job you're after, this is a sure-fire way to boost your employability.

■ Workplace training

If you are currently in a job, it's a good plan to start by finding out what training opportunities your existing employer might be able to offer before going on to explore options elsewhere. If you don't ask, you won't get.

There are all kinds of qualifications you can acquire in the workplace – everything from improving basic numeracy and literacy skills to gaining National Vocational Qualifications (NVQs, which are awarded for competence in work-based activities) and studying at degree level. Look on your company's in-house computer network (if it has one), or ask the human resources (HR) department or your manager if you are eligible. Training methods vary from organization to organization, and can include everything from internal and external conferences, workshops and events to instructor-led training, coaching by external practitioners and online learning.

■ Help your employer to help you

If your organization doesn't offer the training you want, it might be persuaded to fund you, either fully or in part, or allow you some time in the working week to study. If you're not sure what you might want to study, the Employer's Guide to Training Providers (accessed through the Learning and Skills Council's website (**www.lsc.gov.uk**) is a useful resource.

■ Organize your own training

If your new career in the making requires a professional or vocational qualification, or you just want to give yourself an edge over other applicants, you will need to take charge of your own learning. It is important to do detailed research on the area of work that interests you in order to make sure that furthering your education will pay dividends. This includes checking with potential employers that the qualification you have in mind is exactly the right one for the job you want.

Before you sign up for anything, be honest with yourself about whether you will have the staying power to finish the course. Drop-out rates in adult education are high, largely because people take the wrong course or underestimate the necessary commitment. When you are making your plans, consider whether you are sufficiently self-disciplined to study at home. If you think you lack staying power or that other activities will impinge on your time, consider options such as part-time study or online distance learning.

■ Different ways to study

If you want to learn something, there is no lack of opportunity to do so. But how can you fit studying into a busy working life with all your other commitments? Well, the educators have thought of that too, and there's a range of study methods for you to choose from:

- Part-time day study
- Part-time evening study
- Short course study
- Day or block release study
- Customized study
- Distance learning online
- Home study or correspondence courses
- Full-time study

To help you choose the appropriate method of study, think about:

- What time and finance you can afford.
- What your learning style is. Are you are a practical, hands-on type of person, or do you enjoy sitting in a class?
- Are you self-disciplined enough to study independently from home via a correspondence course or through the Open University?
- Have conventional teaching methods suited you in the past?
- Do you need an ordered approach to having information delivered to you, or do you prefer a freer, less structured approach?
- Do you want interaction with other students?

- Are you happy taking end-of-year exams, or would you feel less pressured in a continual assessment environment?
- Are you ready to take time to acquire the qualifications you need, or would a more intense approach to studying be better?
- Can you take a sabbatical from work to enable you to dedicate yourself fully to studying?

If you visit **www.learndirect-advice.co.uk/findacourse/**, you can enter a course name, fill in a location and it will call up a list of possible solutions to match your given criteria.

The time you can make available will probably play a large part in which type of study would suit you best, so have a look at the useful time planner on **www.bbc.co.uk/learning/returning/learninglives/time** to compare the options. And check out **www.direct.gov.uk/EducationAndLearning/ AdultLearning**, which has a useful 'Learning to suit your lifestyle' section.

Getting started

Once you have given some thought to how much time you can devote to studying and what sort of learning style might suit you, the next stage is to pinpoint your area of study.

- **Choose a subject** – depending on the qualification you are seeking, you may study the same thing for several years, so make sure it's something you enjoy.
- **Decide what level of course you want to take** – this will largely be dictated by your current level of education and the minimum job requirements.
- **Choose an institution at which to study** – with home study and online distance learning through many UK institutions, your chosen college need not be close to home.

What qualifications can I study for?

There is now a wide range of qualifications for adults to choose from, both academic and vocational. Obviously, your choice will depend on the qualifications you already have and the requirements of the job sector you want to work in.

- **Access/Foundation courses** – aimed at adults who want to study but don't have the necessary qualifications to get into higher education. They are an ideal way to get back into the study habit.
- **Apprenticeships** – these are mainly for school and college leavers aged 16–24. There are two levels of apprenticeship in 80 different sectors of industry, gained through combinations of Key Skills, NVQs and technical certificates. View a complete list at **www.apprenticeships.org.uk**.
- **BTEC courses** – often taken as an alternative to A levels, and available in a wide range of vocational subjects. Like A levels, a BTEC National Diploma is not a higher education qualification in itself, but it will facilitate your entry into higher education.
- **Business English Certificate (BEC)** – an English-language examination that tests your ability to communicate in English in real-world business situations. BEC exams are offered at three levels, depending on your ability. These are Preliminary (BEC 1), Vantage (BEC 2) and Higher (BEC 3).
- **City & Guilds qualifications** – 500 vocational qualifications from basic to advanced levels in job sectors ranging from hairdressing to bricklaying, and catering to auto repair (see **www.cityandguilds.com**).
- **Foundation degrees** – these are vocational higher education qualifications designed with the help of employers. Blending academic and work based learning, they provide students with specialist technical skills at the associate professional and higher technician level. Courses include accounting and finance, forensic science, police studies and veterinary nursing.
- **Higher Education Awards** – these are Higher National Diplomas (HNDs) and Higher National Certificates (HNCs), work-related courses, including marketing, engineering, horticulture and tourism, that can be used as a route to a degree. An HNC can be studied full-time (one year) or part-time (two years), while an HND takes two years on a full-time basis, or can be structured to study part time over a longer period.
- **Higher Education Diplomas** – two-year courses offered in a range of professional subjects, such as nursing, engineering and textile design.
- **First degrees** – university courses that lead to a qualification such as a Bachelor of Arts (BA) or Bachelor of Science (BSc). These usually takes three or four years to complete and can be studied full-time, part-time or through distance learning.

- **Key Skills** – these form part of apprenticeships (see **www.bbc.co.uk/skillswise**). There are six skills: communication, application of numbers, information communication technology (ICT), working with others, improving own learning and problem solving. Acquiring these skills makes it easier for an employer to gauge your basic abilities.

- **National First Certificates or Diplomas** – these encompass several qualifications and, depending on the level you attain, equate to GCSEs or A levels. They are Ordinary National Certificate/Diploma (ONC or OND), Advanced Vocational Certificate of Education (AVCE) or General National Vocational Qualification (GNVQ). The range of available topics is wide, including computing, health studies, sports education and childcare.

- **Postgraduate awards** – these encompass master's degrees (MA, MBA, MSc, MPhil) and doctorates (PhD). They have no universal standard or content, and the period of study varies.

- **Professional qualifications** – specific courses or exams of various levels undertaken to operate in a particular profession, such as medicine, accountancy, architecture or the law.

Where to get more information

There are many useful websites that offer help and advice about where to go for training courses and further education. Here is a selection.

www.aimhigher.ac.uk – provides lots of information about getting started on the road into higher education.

www.deni.gov.uk – the official site for the Department of Education in Northern Ireland.

www.direct.gov.uk/EducationAndLearning – offers general information on finding and applying for a course.

www.hero.ac.uk/uk/studying/choosing_a_course257.cfm – the Higher Education and Research Opportunities (HERO) website takes you to all the various higher education options and has links to useful websites, including those of UK universities and colleges.

www.hesa.ac.uk – the Higher Education Statistics Agency offers access to all university and higher education college websites. The 'Studying' section of the site is useful.

www.learndirect.co.uk – offers national learning advice for thousands of courses, not just LearnDirect ones.

www.nextstep.org.uk – this should be the first step for adults who have yet to achieve their first full Level 2 qualification (see comparison table on page 122). Local staff can help identify the essential skills you need to improve your job prospects.

www.sfeu.ac.uk – the site for the Scottish Further Education Unit.

www.ucas.ac.uk – the Universities and Colleges Admissions Service (UCAS) is the central organization through which applications are processed for entry to full-time higher education.

www.wfc.ac.uk/education/hefcw/inst.html – offers access to higher education institutions in Wales.

www.worktrain.gov.uk – helps you to search for training in your area.

■ Qualification comparison

The numerous vocational qualifications currently available can be studied in a variety of ways, and have changed over the years. The table below compares the various levels and how they are viewed by employers.

Level	Academic qualification	Vocational qualification equivalent
Below Level 1	Wordpower or Numberpower Basic or Key Skills	
1	GCSEs/O levels with grades D–G CSEs with grades below 1 1 AS level	BEC General Certificate/ Diploma BTEC First Certificate City & Guilds Operative GNVQ Foundation NVQ Level 1 RSA Elementary/First Level

Level	Academic qualification	Vocational qualification equivalent
2	5 or more GCSEs/O levels with grades A–C CSEs grade 1 1 A level 2–3 AS levels	BEC General Cert/Diploma with Credit BTEC First Diploma City & Guilds Higher Operative/Craft GNVQ Intermediate NVQ Level 2 RSA Diploma
3	2 or more A levels 4 or more AS levels	BEC National ONC/OND BTEC National ONC/OND City & Guilds Advanced Craft GNVQ Advanced NVQ Level 3 RSA Advanced Diploma
4	Teaching qualification First degree (BA, BSc)	BEC National HND/HNC BTEC National HND/HNC Higher Education Certificate/ Diploma NVQ Level 4 RSA Higher Diploma
5	Postgraduate degree (MA)	Continuing Education Diploma NVQ Level 5 Other higher level/professional qualifications

■ Funding your study

For comprehensive student funding information visit the Higher Education and Research Opportunities (HERO) website: **www.hero.ac.uk/uk/studying/ funding_your_study/sources_of_help.cfm**. This offers detailed advice on what funds you might be entitled to and the fees you might expect to pay, plus information on access funds and agreements, grants, scholarships, benefits, disabled allowances, career development loans, help with childcare and dependents, and part-time working.

The Educational Grants Advisory Service (EGAS) offers guidance and advice on funding for those studying in post-16 education in the UK. It publishes a *Guide to Student Funding*: **www.egas-online.org**.

The Department for Education and Skills (DfES) Student Support website is at **www.dfes.gov.uk**. The DfES booklet *Money to Learn* tells you what you need to know about getting financial support while studying.

Scholarships are a possible source of funding, and Hot Courses at **www.scholarship-search.org.uk** has a database of all those available to undergraduates.

■ Key points

- A shortage of skilled job applicants is the main reason that employers struggle to fill job vacancies.
- Updating your skills and/or qualifications will make you more appealing to employers.
- Thoroughly research which qualifications will be of most use to you in your chosen career before you select a course.
- Be honest with yourself about the level of commitment you can make to studying before you start.

Statistically, the more employers you contact, the more likely you are to succeed.

Chapter 12
Successful job-hunting

In this chapter you will find:

❏ Why aren't jobs advertised?

❏ Recruitment and employment agencies

❏ Networking on the net

❏ Job-search sites

Having read this far, you will now know a lot more about what you want out of your working life than you did when you started. You will have thought about the sort of job you want and the type of organization you would like to work for, and will have got your head round what employers are looking for and whether you need to update your skills or not. Now it is time to go job-hunting.

In this chapter we are going to start with traditional job-hunting methods and how they can help you to track down the job vacancies you are looking for, and then move on to online job-searching.

- **Answer advertisements** – try national, regional and local papers, trade journals and free newspapers. Depending on what kind of job you are looking for, don't forget shops and newsagents' windows.
- **Register with agencies** – these include general employment agencies, specialist recruitment firms, headhunters and executive agencies, many of which tend to concentrate on a particular job sector or market.
- **Network** – approach employers via friends or contacts in the trade or profession you wish to work in. Some companies actively prefer recruiting via their existing staff, which is why you should always ask around.
- **Conduct market research** – this is slightly different from networking, in that you don't overtly ask for employment. Instead, ask to watch people at work and request an informational interview with the employer. This helps you to develop contacts and gather knowledge of the sector while at the same time alerting a potential employer to your availability.
- **Make speculative approaches** – this is also referred to as 'cold-calling'. You contact an organization directly to see if they have vacancies, or offer your CV for consideration as and when any suitable roles become available.
- **Use an outplacement service** – such services have long been offered to staff being made redundant. Some provide only basic assistance, such as helping you to brush up your CV. However, others offer more intensive help, such as career counselling, life coaching, or direct referrals to other organizations looking to recruit.

■ Why aren't jobs advertised?

Job-seekers sometimes complain that they never even get the chance to compete for the best posts because at least half of them are never openly advertised in the first place. When you think about it, you realize this can't be true. If half of all vacancies weren't publicized in some way, employers would never fill them. What people really mean when they say this is that they never saw the jobs in newspaper ads.

Display advertising in most papers costs a fortune and can produce huge numbers of inappropriate applications that take ages to wade through. That's why many organizations start by listing jobs on their websites or online. They will also approach known associates, existing temporary workers, contractors, or people working for suppliers with whom they have already had dealings. Firms frequently ask their existing employees to recommend candidates. In some cases they even pay cash bonuses if a suitable new employee is subsequently hired.

No wonder research has repeatedly shown that simply responding to newspaper advertisements is not the best job-seeking strategy. You should aim to use at least three different search methods or you will miss out on opportunities simply because you never get to hear of them.

■ What kind of job-hunting works best?

Surprisingly, there's little definitive research on which job-hunting methods achieve the highest success rates. That's why, once you have picked a job field, you must immediately make it your business to find out how people doing those jobs found out about them.

The online recruitment company Jobsite found that 55 per cent of its job-seekers found work via the internet, compared to 22 per cent who answered newspaper ads, 18 per cent who got their jobs through word of mouth, and five per cent who used the trade press. This is, however, a somewhat self-selecting group, which is most likely to use the web and take jobs with large firms.

Research by the UK Office of National Statistics in 2001 revealed that one in ten of all jobs in the UK were found through recruitment consultancies. This, needless to say, is an average figure: the percentage would vary enormously according to the job sector.

Asking friends for job-leads, doing homework on potential firms or organizations, and knocking on their doors can have high success rates, especially for people with skills and qualifications to offer. Such methods are known to be generally more effective than randomly posting your CV, responding to advertisements in national newspaper and trade journals, or even using an employment or recruitment agency.

If you have few formal skills to offer, you will get far better results if you seek advice from a suitably trained adviser, and have the mutual support of other similar job-seekers. Job clubs provide just this kind of cooperative environment: your local jobcentre (**www.jobcentreplus.gov.uk**) should be able to point you in the right direction. If nothing is available locally, it's worth seeing if you can make contact with others in a similar situation.

■ Finding work is a full-time job

Your job-search is unlikely to progress very fast or very far unless you tackle the task with vigour – as if it's a full-time job. Studies for the UK government found that, on average, unemployed people spend fewer than five hours a week actively looking for work. That's not nearly long enough – and here's why. Let's suppose that it takes you six months to find the job you want. If you got yourself organized and managed to devote six hours a day to the task, consistently researching, phoning, visiting organizations and employers, you could have achieved the same outcome in just one month.

■ Find as many potential employers as you can

The best way of getting a feel for different jobs is by spending time with people who do the work in which you're interested. To find them don't overlook traditional directories, such as *Yellow Pages* and *Thomson*. These still have some of the most comprehensive lists of firms in your area, from acupuncture clinics to zinc metal producers.

First, draw up the longest list of target organizations that you can. The more, the better, though it's usually the smaller ones that are more likely to recruit informally.

The next step is to visit or make direct contact with every company on your list. Call up each one and say you are thinking of entering their field. Ask if they'd mind letting you watch what they do for a day. Many may refuse, so you will need to approach as many as you possibly can.

■ Apply for jobs before they are advertised

This kind of uninvited job-hunting or 'cold calling' uses a combination of phone calls, email or letters and is all about striking it lucky – managing to make your approach just when a vacancy may be arising, but nothing has yet been done about it. Staff resign, get fired, are promoted, take maternity leave, become ill or even die. The firm has a problem, but you are the solution that's just walked in through the door.

You may need to do some online detective work to discover the name and title of the exact person who does the hiring in your field. Then it's a question of emailing or writing to that named individual, enclosing your CV, and asking if you could see them briefly to discuss any present or future job openings. This process is a little easier if you have done some prior networking and can drop the name of someone who suggested you get in touch. If they say yes, ask for a 15-minute informational interview, and stick to that time.

■ It takes persistence

If you end up with a name to contact but no email details, look online and see if you can find the address of at least one person in the company. The way their name is spelt out with initials or dots should allow you to figure out the likely address of the person you are trying to reach. When your messages are no longer bounced back, that usually means you have reached your target.

To get a face-to-face meeting, you will almost certainly have to follow up your initial approach on the phone, perhaps trying to get through at different times of the day. Some employers respond better if you have first sent a letter, but don't get upset if they claim to have lost it, or not even to have seen it. Be persistent, but never rude or pushy.

■ Be creative

If you get to see someone, it's important to demonstrate how you would be of positive benefit if you were taken on. For example, you might have read that the operation is expanding or has won new business, in which case you could outline what expertise you have that they might be short of. You could draw on your past experience to come up with some ideas to bring in more business. Above all, leave a good impression because you want to be the first person they think of if a post becomes available. Sometimes jobs are especially created for impressive candidates. Statistically, the more employers you contact, the more likely you are to succeed.

■ Ask plenty of questions

Once you get an informational interview, don't forget that you are in the driving seat. Have a notebook with your key questions already written down and take notes. Ask things such as:

- What qualifications do you have and how did you get the job?
- What do you do in a typical day?
- What sort of decisions do you take?
- What are the best and worst aspects of the job?
- What do you look for in new applicants?
- How are people trained and appraised?
- What's the work culture like: do you often stay late, is it formal or informal, do people work without close supervision?
- What areas are expanding or might offer future opportunities?
- What do people do to get on here?
- Would you look over my CV and tell me if I lack skills or experience?
- Who else should I talk to?

In assessing the suitability of a job, remember that some employers are skilled at putting a gloss on what they do, making advertised posts look exciting in recruitment advertising or on their websites. Some even include 'testimonials' from carefully selected existing employees – best taken with a pinch of salt. Approach any of this material as you would a holiday brochure, looking as carefully for what it doesn't say as for what it does. That's why it's so useful to talk directly with people who have worked for the firm: it helps to form a more accurate impression of what it's really like.

■ Job fairs are full of ideas

Another way of sizing up potential employers is by attending job fairs or exhibitions, often held by groups of firms in the same sector or industry. If you have little experience approaching employers and you especially want to impress one exhibitor, don't head straight there: nerves might overcome you. Better to make a few practice runs with others first. Use some of the questions and interviewing tips mentioned earlier in this chapter. Always ask for a business card and make brief notes of what was said. Then, when applying for work, you can mention your earlier conversation.

■ Using recruitment and employment agencies

Depending on your field, agencies can open doors for you. If you use them to land a full-time job, they are usually paid a generous fee by the client company, so they should be naturally motivated to find you work. Try to choose an established agency with a good reputation that's used by people already working in the area you want to get into. Test them out by asking to see the current vacancies on offer.

Much will hang on the quality of the registration process and initial interview. Detailed account should be taken of your career objectives, preferences, availability and salary needs. Treat your initial contact with the agency as you would a normal job interview. They won't bother referring you to employers if you are untidy, offhand or unclear about what you want to do. Ask them directly what your chances are, and get feedback if you are not successful.

Don't reject short-term work out of hand. Temporary assignments can last from one day to a year or more, and although some may be dead-end jobs, others could blossom quite unexpectedly into longer-term assignments, even offers of permanent employment.

With a few exceptions, mainly in the fields of entertainment and modelling, UK law prevents agencies charging for finding or trying to find you work. They must give you their terms in writing, and must pay you, even if they have not been paid by an employer. Choose an agency that caters for the types of job in which you are interested.

■ Online job-hunting

The recruitment world moves fast, so if you don't have access to the internet, you will find it difficult to keep updated about the jobs that are available. Getting your own computer and modem is something you should seriously think about organizing if you possibly can. However, there are internet cafés on most high streets now, or you can register with your local library and gain free use of their computers and internet facilities for limited periods of time.

Organizations choose to use the net because they find it cheaper and quicker than advertising in print. Most also post vacancies on their own websites, which costs them almost nothing. You can research your target employers, contact them by email, and zap off your CV at the touch of a mouse. (You can also waste a lot of time getting sidetracked down blind cyber-alleys, so it is not a bad idea to limit the number of hours you spend on this sort of search.)

■ Networking on the net

The World Wide Web isn't just a good place to look for advertised posts: it's where people of like minds meet, and is opening up new avenues for networking. Professional organizations have always been among the best places for researching and finding job-leads. Now all these communities of employers and individuals with similar interests can be found online. There are also tens of thousands of discussion groups, newsgroups and forums all over the net, and quite a few of these are dedicated to jobs. Find out which ones are used by people in your field of interest and see if you can join them. When you do, don't forget to ask all the people with whom you come into contact which job sites they have found most useful.

■ Job-search sites

Online recruitment has been through a big shake-up since the dot.com boom and bust. Many small sites have been amalgamated into larger ones, which has slightly reduced the number you will need to check out. Many are operated by large newspaper groups, which once dominated the market for classified job advertisements.

The best job-search sites supplement their listings with 'knowledge zones', which often include CV advice, interview tips and online psychometric testing, as well as links to external sites that offer paid advice.

By the way, if you're thinking of spending your lunch hour at work quietly surfing a few job sites, look out for ones such as that operated by the *Daily Telegraph*, which provides a panic button. This allows you quickly to navigate to an innocuous website and avoid being caught out looking for a new job if your manager unexpectedly walks past your monitor.

■ Where should I start my online search?

If you currently possess only basic skills, the **www.jobcentreplus.gov.uk** and **www.worktrain.gov.uk** sites have jobs databases. The 'Futures' initiative on the **www.learndirect.co.uk** site, is also a good starting point.

The biggest problem facing graduate-level or skilled people with work experience is the sheer number of online job sites. Work and job-related sites have proliferated at such a rate in recent years that it has become impossible to visit them all, let alone evaluate them.

But you have to start somewhere, so we have tried to make the task easier for you by asking experienced researchers to assess a large number of job sites and draw up a list of those they rated highest. Of course, sites come and go, and some start well only to lose their edge after a while. But at the time of writing, we feel that the ones on our list are worth a visit because they are not only user-friendly, but should also prove a productive use of your time.

Most are general job sites, but some specialist ones are included in the list on pages 134–135 because they scored highly and cover numerous areas you might want to explore. Our researchers visited many more job sites than those listed here, and scored each category out of ten.

The list gives a general idea of how good the job descriptions, search facilities and job-type groupings are on each site, as well as distinguishing between those sites that focus on just job listings and those that are more interactive. Some allow recruiters to browse your CV. This last point is important because you will need to make frequent return visits to those sites that do not allow you to post your CV to check for new vacancies on offer.

■ Appearances can be deceptive

Incidentally, although the appearance of sites inevitably influences how appealing you initially find them, we did find a lot of great-looking sites that were actually difficult to use because they were so bugged with non-functional searches and dead-ends. Appearances can therefore be deceptive, so you should be aware that some of the most useful sites are not necessarily the most stylishly designed.

Best job sites for graduates and skilled workers

Site	Number of jobs	Categorized?	Specialist?	Clear & helpful?	List of employers	CV help	CV posting	Interview technique?	Tests	Inter-national	Search	Email alerts
www.appointments-plus.co.uk[1]	250	9	No	8	Yes	No	No	No	Yes	Yes	9	Yes
www.bigbluedog.co.uk	8,800	8	No, but London bias	8	Yes	No	Yes	No	No	No	8	Yes
www.computerweekly.co.uk	300	7	IT professionals	9	Yes	No	No	No	No	Yes	7	Yes
www.dotjobs.co.uk	50	6	Printing and packaging industry	7	No	No	No	No	No	No	5	Yes
www.fish4jobs.co.uk	37,500	7	No	7	No	Yes	Yes	No	Yes	Yes	9	Yes
www.gisajob.co.uk	29,000	8	No	9	No	No	Yes	No	No	Yes	7	Yes
www.jobs.ac.uk[2]	2,500	9	Science, academia and related professions	8	Yes	No	No	No	No	Yes	9	Yes
www.jobserve.com[3]	45,000	9	No	8	Yes	No	Yes	No	No	Yes	9	Yes
www.jobtrack.co.uk	21,000	7	No	8	Yes	No	Yes	No	No	Yes	8	Yes
www.jobsunlimited.co.uk[4]	7,000	9	No	8	Yes	Yes	No	Yes	Yes	Yes	9	Yes

Site	Number of jobs	Categorized?	Specialist?	Clear & helpful?	List of employers	CV help	CV posting	Interview technique?	Tests	International	Search	Email alerts
www.jobswithballs.com[5]	200	9	Sport and leisure industry	8	No	Yes	Yes	Yes	No	Yes	8	Yes
www.jobworld.co.uk[6]	14,000	7	Computing & IT	8	Yes	Yes	Yes	Yes	Yes	Yes	9	Yes
www.lgjobs.com	1,600	8	Local government jobs in the UK	8	No	No	No	No	No	No	7	Yes
www.monster.co.uk	41,000	9	No	11	Yes	Yes	Yes	Yes	Yes	Yes	8	Yes
www.newscientistjobs.com	1,600	9	Jobs in science	3	Yes	Yes	Yes	No	No	Yes	8	Yes
www.reed.co.uk	243,000	9	No	8	No	Yes	Yes	Yes	Yes	Yes	9	Yes
www.s1jobs.com	7,000	8	Jobs in Scotland	7	Yes	Yes	Yes	Yes	No	No	7	Yes
www.topjobs.net[7]	800	9	No	8	Yes	No	No	No	No	Yes	7	Yes
www.totaljobs.com	87,000	8	No	3	Yes	Yes	Yes	Yes	Yes	Yes	8	Yes
www.uk.careers.yahoo.com	40,000	7	No	7	Yes	No	No	No	No	Yes	8	Yes

[1] This site is operated by the *Daily Telegraph*. A notable feature is the panic button
[2] This is run by the University of Warwick
[3] This site has been operating since 1993
[4] This site is run by the *Guardian*
[5] In operation since the end of 2003
[6] This site has changed its name to www.computingcareers.co.uk
[7] This site has a special service for PDAs

■ Key points

- Most firms use a variety of methods to find staff before resorting to expensive newspaper advertising. Find out how jobs are typically advertised in your field.

- Many of the best job-seeking methods involve networking and knocking on doors. Use more than one method and devote yourself full time to the task to raise your chances of success.

- Plan your meetings with people to get the most out of each encounter, and ask for more contacts to extend your search.

- Choose recruitment agencies with a good track record and present yourself to them professionally, as if you were attending a full job interview.

- Your online job-search will be less effective if you do not have high-speed internet access.

- You can use the internet to network with other people in your chosen field of work, as well as to search for jobs.

- Approach your online job-search in a structured way or you run the risk of wasting hours of time in random surfing.

The main reason optimists fare better than pessimists is because of the way they deal with setbacks.

Chapter 13
Positive thinking

In this chapter you will find:

❑ How to be happier

❑ Dealing with negative baggage

❑ Setbacks

You don't need to be a genius to work out that you're far more likely to succeed in making your move into a more rewarding career if you set about it with a positive mindset.

Is the glass half-full or half-empty?

Would you describe yourself as an optimist or a pessimist? Most of us are a bit of both, depending on the circumstances. But it's a highly relevant question because research suggests that optimists are generally more successful than pessimists.

Studies carried out at the University of Pennsylvania in the USA concluded that the main reason optimists fare better than pessimists is to do with the way they deal with setbacks. When they run into difficulties, optimists generally regard these as only temporary. Pessimists, on the other hand, do the opposite, seeing setbacks as long term and far-reaching – or even permanent. This, in turn, can make them feel so defeated that they can't see the point of trying to find solutions. By contrast, optimists manage to deal with their setbacks and are able to move on to future successes.

So what's the lesson here? Well, we're not suggesting that you approach every challenge you meet in a spirit of unrealistic euphoria. But it is worth recognizing that your state of mind when you approach a hurdle can have a direct impact on your chances of getting over it. If you suspect that you have fallen into the habit of thinking negatively, here are some simple but surprisingly effective tips for developing a more positive attitude.

How to be happier

- When you wake up, make a mental commitment to be happy.
- Deliberately look on the bright side, and find reasons to smile more often.
- Have faith in yourself and your abilities.
- Don't waste time on negative thoughts, doubts or worries.
- Spend as much time as you can with positive, happy people.
- Focus on your goals and how you are going to achieve them.
- Look forward – don't dwell on the past.

■ Negative baggage

Even if you're feeling confident and optimistic about finding a new career, it's worth giving some thought as to whether you're still carrying mental baggage that you need to leave behind. For example, you might have failed in a previous attempt to make a career change, and now a fear of failure may be lurking in your mind, unconsciously holding you back. Or perhaps you left your last job in unhappy circumstances and are still harbouring a sense of resentment – perhaps a feeling that your bosses *always* treat you badly. You might feel that you're somehow *owed* better luck next time.

Maybe you've had a series of jobs that didn't work out as you hoped, and you feel that you're jinxed in some way. Only you know exactly what happened, and perhaps you were in no way to blame. Nonetheless, you should ask yourself whether your behaviour in those jobs contributed *in any way* to the problems you had.

Negative behaviour can creep up on all of us. Examine your work history honestly and look at how you responded to challenges and tricky situations or individuals along the way. You might start to spot some repeating patterns; for instance, maybe you haven't been as flexible as you could have. Perhaps you avoided taking on more responsibilities when the opportunity arose. Have you made unreasonable demands of your colleagues or subordinates? Did you acknowledge mistakes you made and learn from them? Could you have been more proactive and enthusiastic?

A bit of honest soul-searching now can genuinely improve your chances of enjoying your work more in future. You don't have to dwell on any of the nasty or embarrassing stuff you come up with: simply recognize it as behaviour you want to change in your new career. And hold that thought because the longer you have been repeating negative patterns, the tougher you will find it to break the habit and the more likely you are to relapse.

■ Setbacks

Managing a job change can feel like an almost impossible task, not least because you'll probably to have to deal with some (if not all) of the following problems:

■ Your initial enthusiasm for a move fades and you lose motivation.
■ You can't seem to decide what sort of work you want to do.

- When you start to research the careers you're attracted to, they all seem tougher to get into than you ever expected.
- You start to wonder if you're too old.
- You start to doubt your own abilities.
- People you approach for help aren't as helpful or supportive as you hoped.
- You apply for jobs but can't even get an interview.
- You go for job interviews but don't receive any job offers.
- The process takes far longer than you expected, and even your friends and family stop asking how you're getting on.

Don't panic. Setbacks are to be expected – they're a normal part of the process. Unless you're extraordinarily highly motivated, there are going to be times when you wonder why you're putting in all this time and effort to achieve something so elusive. The important thing is to stick at it. Set aside a period of time each day when you will fully devote yourself to the business of your career change. What you do in that time depends on where you are in the process. It might be appropriate to spend a couple of hours reading this book; surfing the net for more information about particular careers or education opportunities; researching or visiting organizations or individuals who might be able to help you; looking for suitable vacancies; emailing contacts or writing letters. Whatever it is, don't allow yourself to put it off.

■ Five common delaying tactics

Research by psychologists in Canada suggests that not getting on with tasks you know you should be tackling induces more stress than doing the tasks in the first place. The researchers identified five kinds of what they termed 'faulty thinking' which tend to lead to procrastination:

1. I can work only when I'm in the mood.
2. I need to like the task in hand.
3. I have to complete the task in one go.
4. I have plenty of time to get it done.
5. I work better under pressure, so everything should be left until the last minute.

Sound familiar? Getting a new career off the ground is like taking exams or losing weight: other people can help you, but no one else can actually do it for you. You may love the idea of succeeding, but the day-to-day reality of putting in the necessary work can be tedious and demanding. If you doubt your own ability to knuckle down, find a friend or a colleague to act as your conscience. Schedule a weekly conversation with them about what you want to achieve next and the progress you've made. Don't pick someone who will let you off if you haven't put in the work; you need someone who will be tough with you.

If you find you have done something else when you should have been working on your next job, make a commitment to put the time you took out back into your career change project *the next day*.

■ Key points

- You are statistically more likely to achieve a successful career move if you set about it in an optimistic frame of mind.
- Be careful not to take negative mental baggage or behaviour with you when you start a new job.
- Expect to run into setbacks as you progress your career change, but do not let them deflect you from your purpose.

It's often said that the outcome of the average job interview is determined in the first 90 seconds.

Chapter 14
Making the right impression

In this chapter you will find:

❏ What makes a good CV

❏ Sample CV

❏ Covering letters

❏ Application forms

❏ Online applications

❏ Assessment centres

First impressions count, and you won't even get through the door of a potential employer unless you can jump through some unavoidable hoops first. Your CV, your completed job application form and any contact by phone or email are all sales tools. If the recruiter likes what he or she sees or hears, then you have your foot in the door.

It's often said that the outcome of the average job interview is determined in the first 90 seconds. What luxury! When it comes to sifting through the pre-interview paperwork, the time spent assessing the merits of each potential applicant is put at less than – wait for it – 20 seconds. That's really all the time you have, so getting that initial approach right is crucial.

To be selected for interview you have to come up with some compelling reasons why you should be given the job. For instance, if you are looking for a post in sales and have previously helped your section increase yearly profit by 30 per cent, that's the kind of information you should highlight. This may sound obvious, but even talented, highly skilled people are not necessarily good at self-promotion. Your best qualities will not speak for themselves: you need to make your abilities crystal clear to the recruiter.

Most employers are trying to discover no more than four things:

1. Does this applicant possess the minimum qualifications?
2. Is the applicant competent to do the job?
3. Does the applicant's track record suggest that he or she will be motivated to do the job effectively?
4. Will the applicant fit within the culture of our organization?

■ Making connections on paper

Your CV, more properly your curriculum vitae (from the Latin, meaning 'course of life'), should be a clear, concise document that sets out and quantifies your achievements for a prospective employer. Too many are poorly structured, long-winded, misspelt and difficult to read. Little wonder, then, that many employers distrust them.

Does your CV spell out every heroic task you have performed since your boss asked you to organize the works awayday to Brighton? Such information is pretty pointless unless you can demonstrate how your achievements will equip you for the job being advertised. While employers need to know what you have done, they are more interested in knowing what you actually made of the jobs you had.

Let's imagine you are applying for a job to run the IT department within a growing business. If you say that you have 'project-managed a computer network upgrade', this is unlikely to win you many Brownie points. However, think through your actual achievements and you might come up with 'personally overcame staff resistance and supervised the adoption of a completely new, office-wide IT system to budget and ahead of schedule'. Now that's more like it!

This example demonstrates that you have not only the ability to get things done, but also the motivation. Similarly, don't claim to have 'supervised new learning programmes to address staff retention problems'. How about: 'made the business case for and initiated NVQ training, which cut annual staff turnover in my section by seven per cent a year'.

Use active and varied language, avoiding jargon and repetition. Don't endlessly repeat the word 'managed' when you can describe how you 'negotiated', 'developed' or 'initiated' a successful project.

If the document you send out to every potential employer is always the same, it's unlikely to be one that will hit the spot. Without personal contact, there's also little point in mass-mailing your CV, unsolicited, to numerous employers. The main exception is for job-seekers who lodge their CVs with agencies recruiting in a specific field, such as IT. These specialist CVs need to be compiled with plenty of keywords describing your expertise, which can be matched to the needs of employers.

One of the biggest benefits of a well-prepared CV is that if you are invited in to discuss things further, it can provide some great talking points for the interviewer to latch on to, and you are more likely to be asked questions you will have prepared for.

Re-evaluating and putting a gloss on your work experience to date is not remotely the same as exaggerating or falsifying your CV. Don't even think about doing the latter. Ever larger numbers of firms employ people to check applicants' claims thoroughly. The moment your sins find you out, you will be shown the door.

■ Strike a chord with employers

CVs are all about presenting your achievements in a way that will strike a chord with potential employers. You need to convey the message that you actively want to work for the company, and aren't just desperate to take any job that may be going.

Always read the published job requirements carefully. In your thought process you will need to deconstruct your past career thoroughly to paint a vivid picture of the unique attributes you have for hire. You should also make yourself aware of the cultural 'feel' of the organization. For example, is it informal, hierarchical, or is it one where individuals are expected to display high levels of autonomy or initiative?

Your CV should be a highly targeted piece of marketing. Just think how annoying it is to get junk mail at home. Indiscriminate, irrelevant mailshots are a waste of everyone's time. To put it another way, you need to show that you are a square peg ready to fit into the square hole that has just opened up.

■ Chronological versus functional CVs

The most familiar kind of CV is usually described as 'chronological', meaning that it gives a straightforward, historical account of what you have done since you left school. After your name and contact details, the five most typical sections are:

- Key skills.
- Employment history.
- Education and training.
- Personal interests.
- Any other relevant information.

Chronological CVs clearly show a candidate's progression up the ladder – for example, from a first job as marketing assistant to being appointed brand manager. It lists your posts by title and date, starting with the most recent and going back in time.

Although this type of CV conveys the facts perfectly well, job-changers tend increasingly to compile what is called a 'functional' CV. This points up your skills and strengths, allowing you to describe yourself through what you have learnt and can offer, rather than majoring on the posts you have held. It's best used if you are applying for a first job, moving into a new field, if you have spent some time out of work, or if you've chopped and changed jobs a lot.

Be warned, however, that some traditional employers remain suspicious of functional CVs, as they can be used to disguise gaps in your work experience. It's therefore important to include a brief summary, with dates, of all your various roles, just to show that you have nothing to hide. (The sample shown on pages 151–152 is a cross between a chronological and a functional CV, so it should satisfy most employers.)

■ What to put in your CV

Start right at the top with your name (in bold type, using a larger font), followed by your full contact details. Then, in just two or three sentences, comes a pithy and positive profile of your attributes, custom tailored to show you are a great fit with the job you are going for. These words tell the employers what they will get if they hire you. Here's a description of someone applying for a job as a senior business development manager:

A self-motivated and enthusiastic business development manager with extensive experience in marketing, budgeting, financial planning and resource management. Demonstrable track record in analytical problem-solving, and proven leadership skills in motivating other staff to achieve company objectives.

Underneath your profile, it's best to use bullet points to summarize your experience, skills and achievements, followed by your formal employment and educational history in reverse chronological order. Relevant hobbies, sporting interests and any other points should go at the end. CVs should show, not tell, what you can do.

List only activities that you are able to discuss knowledgeably, or that demonstrate something positive, such as a desire to keep fit, or the ability to lead a team. Bear in mind that an interviewer over, say, 40 may not be impressed by someone who spends all his or her spare time going clubbing, playing computer games or fantasy role-playing.

Make the best of your professional accomplishments, but do ensure that everything you say can be substantiated. Avoid excessive use of adjectives and jargon, which will only irritate the reader.

It's not usually necessary to name people who will give you a reference: you might choose different referees depending on the job being applied for. Just ensure it's clear that these are readily available on request.

Always use short sentences and active language. This will make it easy for someone to skim your CV and hopefully they will want to see you in person to discover more. The whole CV should fill no more than two A4 pages.

■ Presentation and layout

Whatever you do, don't let yourself down with poor spelling, incorrect grammar or sloppy layout. Get some help from a suitably skilled friend, relative or professional. This includes making sure that your CV is nicely printed on good-quality white paper. It's no longer acceptable to use a typewriter or to write it all out by hand.

Don't be tempted to use fancy fonts, paper or bindings that will distract from the content. Many companies do a roaring trade helping people to compose their CVs, offering, in some cases, to send out your details to potential employers. While professionally produced CVs can look impressive, they do not always ring true, so think hard before going down that avenue.

Few CVs are perfect, and that includes the sample on pages 151–152, which is reprinted by kind permission of **www.careers-scotland.org.uk**. This is one of the many websites where useful CV and other careers advice can be found. No single style works for everyone, but we liked the way this example manages to follow the general format of the more modern functional CV without losing sight of the candidate's full career history. See what you think.

■ Mind the gap

Unfortunately, most employers don't rate time spent travelling or bringing up children as highly as experience clocked up in employment. Nevertheless, don't attempt to hide such gaps in your work experience. What you should do instead is draw attention to your personal achievements, noting, for example, any charitable or community involvement you might have had. Ask friends what you are good at – you might be surprised by their answers. Perhaps you could show how you reached a particular goal by galvanizing or organizing others. If you have been looking after children, you will probably have developed good communication, negotiation or time-management skills, which you will need to spell out.

Stephen Black

16 House Avenue
Craigairn
KY7 5NS
Telephone: 075920 109132
Email: sb@hotmail.com

An excellent multi-skilled engineer, with broad experience in management, planning, plant operation and maintenance roles, together with good administration skills.

SKILLS & EXPERIENCE

• Experienced in commissioning newly installed and overhauled equipment.
• Can effectively manage multi skilled teams of staff, including allocating, activating and monitoring their work assignments, ensuring compliance with Health & Safety standards, training and carrying out performance appraisals.
• High level of competency in mechanical system and control troubleshooting, analysing problems and developing solutions.
• Skilled in preparing operating procedures and safe systems of work for tools and equipment.
• Assisted in the establishment of a Local Area Network using a combination of Windows NT4 and Windows 2000 operating systems.

EMPLOYMENT HISTORY

REID ENGINEERING, ROSYTH   May 1992–August 1998
PROJECT MANAGER   June 1994–August 1998
• Ensured work was completed on time and within budget.
• Allocated staff and equipment to projects as required.
• Ensured work was conducted in compliance with Health & Safety regulations.
• Liaised with internal and external contractors to provide additional resources/support.
• Attended fortnightly management team meetings to advise on progress of a variety of projects.
• Inspected work and signed work completion certification.

PROJECT ENGINEER   May 1992–June 1994

• Directly supervised electrical and mechanical fitters and other tradesmen employed on a variety of naval contracts.

• Advised project managers and management team on progress of work.

• Problem-solving/troubleshooting to minimize delays to work.

• Authorized ordering of relevant parts and equipment from the stores.

• Completed workforce timesheets and maintained work schedules.

FAILSAFE ENGINEERING, BURNTISLAND   June 1984–May 1992

MECHANICAL FITTER/SUPERVISOR   January 1989–May 1992

• Supervised team of six mechanical fitters.

• Installed generators, pumps and hydraulic motors in ships and barges.

• Stripped down and serviced the above either on site or in the workshop.

• Completed any other mechanical work as directed.

APPRENTICE FITTER   June 1984–January 1989

• Completed four-year mechanical engineering apprenticeship.

EDUCATION & TRAINING

POSTGRADUATE CERTIFICATE IN MANAGEMENT (1998–99)

Napier University (Distance Learning)

Edinburgh

PROJECT MANAGEMENT COURSE (May 1998)

Reid Engineering

HEALTH & SAFETY FOR MANAGERS (April 1996)

Reid Engineering

FIRST AID COURSE (four days, December 1991)

Mines Rescue, Crossgates

CITY & GUILDS IN MECHANICAL ENGINEERING (1984–88)

Fife College

ADDITIONAL INFORMATION

• Clean driving licence for HGV, car and motorcycle.

• MOD forklift truck operator's certificate.

• Trained in first aid.

• Any employer offering me employment could be eligible for up to £1000 in training grants.

REFERENCES

Excellent testimonials available on request.

■ Write a good covering letter

Having spent hours honing your CV, don't spoil the effect with a sloppy covering letter. Try to find out whom you should address the application to, and start by stating exactly which job you are applying for. In the body of the text, respond directly to the job demands spelt out in the advertisement, and demonstrate clearly how you fit the bill. The points you make should draw attention to the detail of your CV. For example, 'As you can see from my CV, my staff training initiative cut annual staff turnover in my section by seven per cent a year.' Make it interesting and don't waffle; remember, you are selling yourself.

■ Application forms

The larger the organization, the more likely it is to use standardized forms aimed at making the selection process fairer and more transparent. The people invited for interview will be those whose qualifications and track record best match the stated job requirements.

Few people enjoy completing job applications. Some find the prospect so intimidating or time-consuming that they don't even bother to try. But the task does become less daunting once you settle down and consider the form one section at a time.

Many companies use computers to read your application – one reason why you should never start filling in the actual form until you are sure you have your responses exactly right and can fill it in neatly. Make photocopies of the original so that you can practise, and ask a friend or relative to look through your answers (a fresh pair of eyes will notice things that you miss). Keep filed and dated copies of all your completed forms as they could save you a lot of time gathering information in the future.

Be brutally honest with yourself. If your qualifications and experience don't match the job specifications, you probably won't be asked for interview, so it may not be worth spending time on the application. But if you think you do have what it takes, never assume you aren't in with a good chance – even if you know large numbers of people will apply. Typically, many forms will be rejected because they have missed the deadline. Others will fall at the first fence because they are incorrectly completed, or the applicants don't meet the job specifications. Here's how one advisory organization, the Countryside Jobs Service (**www.countryside-jobs.com**), puts things into perspective:

100 people submit application forms for a job, of which

90 will arrive before the closing date, of which

85 will be readable, of which

80 will be completed fully, of which

40 will have all the essential requirements, of which

20 will have most of the desirable requirements, of which

10 will have some additional skills, qualifications or experience, of which .

8 will be invited for interview, of whom

6 will actually attend, of whom

1 will get the job!

■ A word about words

According to researchers at the University of Hertfordshire, choosing the right words can actively help your job application to stand out from the rest. They came up with two lists of words that can sway recruiters, who have to sift through hundreds of forms.

Ten best words

achievement, active, developed, evidence, experience, impact, individual, involved, planning, transferable skills

Ten worst words

always, awful, bad, fault, hate, mistake, never, nothing, panic, problems

As you can see, it's all about avoiding the negative and stressing the positive. For example, talk about the 'valuable lessons' you have learnt rather than going on about your 'mistakes'. Also, avoid over-emphatic words, such as 'never' and 'always', as these can give the impression that you are exaggerating and therefore not entirely believable.

■ Online job applications

Increasing numbers of organizations are using e-application systems that can be accessed through their websites. In fact, some now accept only online applications. This is generally good news because it simplifies the whole process of applying: there are no worries about messy handwriting and your completed application goes straight on to the employer's database without postal delays. Just don't press 'send' until you are absolutely sure your application is complete.

Do beware leaving your online application to the last minute. It's all too easy to work through a web-based form at the eleventh hour, only to find that you will actually miss the deadline because you didn't spot the bit at the end asking you to get references or post other required documents ahead of that date.

Never forget that you are composing a job application, not an email, and you won't get away with rambling replies, slipshod grammar and spelling errors. Remember the four Cs – concise, correct, clear, and conversational. Print off the form first, read it carefully and note down ideas as you work through each section. Prepare any longer answers in a document of your own, using the spell-checker, then cut and paste into the relevant parts of the form. Put your application aside for a while (preferably overnight), then go back to it with fresh eyes for your final proofread, as you are more likely to spot errors you missed.

■ Testing times for job-seekers

Some employers (especially large companies) make use of psychometric or other multiple-choice tests in their selection procedures to whittle down the hefty number of applicants they receive for each post. In most cases, the results are interpreted alongside other information on your CV and application form. Any employer who uses such tests should give you notice, and send practice examples prior to your testing session. Increasingly, tests are conducted online.

Organizations typically use written tests to:

- **See** if an applicant is competent to do the job or likely to acquire the necessary skills.
- **Discover** if a candidate is motivated and in sympathy with the organization.
- **Test** numerical or verbal reasoning, and spatial or diagrammatical awareness.

- **Measure** intellectual capacity for logical thinking.
- **Compare** a candidate's performance with average levels in that role.
- **Look** for certain personal qualities deemed appropriate for the job.
- **Check** technical skills, such as operating machinery and forklift trucks.

Try to relax and respond honestly. If you just give the answers you think the recruiter wants, you will probably end up being inconsistent. Comfort yourself with the thought that if the organization has decided it wants a certain kind of person, the exercises it sets will discover if you are that person. If it turns out that you aren't, there's nothing you can do about it anyway. Equally, if you fail to pass required numeracy or technical tests, it's unlikely you'd thrive in the job.

■ Assessment centres

Some employers recruiting senior staff or graduates find making their final selection is easier if they combine a range of psychometric tests with group interviews, role-playing and impromptu exercises to assess how people perform in different situations. If you are invited to join such a group, it means the employer has shortlisted you, but wants to find out more about your capabilities before making a final decision.

Before you attend, make sure you thoroughly understand the nature of the job on offer, the work that it will involve and the skills and experience it will require – this is what the assessment panel will be measuring you against.

The moment you first walk through the door you will be assessed on your punctuality, appearance, and how you interact and present yourself. Learn everybody's names at the start and use them (in moderation). Otherwise, use your common sense: carefully note any instructions, listen and give credit to others, and try to build a consensus in the group. Summarize suggested solutions and monitor the group's progress against the objectives you have been set. Keep an eye on the clock so that you are ready in time.

- **Group exercises** are designed to test your leadership skills, as well as how you perform as part of a team. Aim to be positive and enthusiastic from the start, but remember that the objective is to win against the competition.

- **Role-playing** requires you to enter into the spirit of your assigned role straight away, whatever your private feelings about the artificiality of the situation. Think about the skills the job requires and demonstrate them.
- **Presentations** are sometimes requested from candidates. Usually short, they require you to prepare information and speak from brief notes or bullet points rather than writing everything out. Few people relish public speaking, but so many jobs call for this ability that it's worth practising.

As to what might count against you – well, not contributing much or remaining aloof in group work won't get you very far. Similarly, interrupting people, failing to listen and being unfair, unkind or overly aggressive will also earn marks against you.

After you have left the assessment centre, take time to reflect on how you performed. If you don't hear anything after a few days, contact the employer and politely request some feedback on your performance.

You may get just the one chance to impress an employer, or you may have to 'set out your stall' over several months in a string of written exchanges and face-to-face interviews. But remember, all the while you will be picking up useful clues that should help you to feel more engaged and feed your enthusiasm.

■ Key points

- Tailor your CV and job application forms to highlight your skills, experience and personal qualities that make you the best candidate for the job.
- Turn detective to track down who recruits staff at organizations that interest you. Give them reasons to interview you face-to-face before any vacancies have actually arisen.
- Don't be put off by psychometric and other tests that employers use to assess your suitability and potential.
- Do as much research as you can to understand how potential employers operate so that you can demonstrate why employing you will make the organization run more effectively.

Working out quickly what lies behind each question will help you to give a good answer.

Chapter 15
How to shine at interviews

In this chapter you will find:

❑ Preparation

❑ What to wear

❑ Relaxation techniques

❑ Assessing an offer

❑ Feedback

Most people say, 'I don't perform well in interviews.' The truth is that many people don't *prepare* well. A job interview is, after all, your opportunity to show an employer what he or she will get if you are appointed. Turning up on time and looking the part is absolutely essential, but so is doing your homework. You need to arrive armed with detailed knowledge of the employer and the field of work you want to enter. You must communicate clearly why you are a shoo-in for the post.

So, before we go any further, what are the most common interview mistakes? Here are 15 of them:

- Inability to express ideas clearly, mumbling and poor grammar.
- Over-enthusiastic, overbearing or aggressive attitude.
- Little vitality, enthusiasm or rapport with the interviewers.
- Being well qualified but lacking 'warmth'.
- Failure to listen.
- Not looking the interviewer(s) in the eye.
- General negativity or overt criticism of a current employer.
- Inability to produce anecdotal examples to support arguments.
- Failure to ask questions or show knowledge of the role or the company.
- Inability to explain reason for leaving current position.
- Inability to explain existing role clearly.
- Inappropriate appearance.
- Wanting too much too soon – unwillingness to start at the bottom.
- Over-emphasis on money.
- Lying or exaggerating achievements.

Preparing for your interview

You can find almost limitless free advice online about handling interviews. When it comes to preparation, however, it is essential to consider the following four areas.

1. Think carefully about the job advertised

What qualifications and skills are being sought? If there's no job description, have you asked for one? Start with the wording of the vacancy, then discover everything you can about the requirements and likely priorities of this particular job. Would elements of the job overstretch you, does it fit you like a glove, or would the work soon bore you?

2. Research the organization offering the job

Look online, in newspapers and trade publications for information about your prospective employer. Consider the issues facing the organization and what differentiates its employees from those of its rivals. How are successful workers rewarded? Do you actively like the sound of the place and the people and feel you would fit in? What would your boss be like?

3. Think about the kind of person they ideally want

What knowledge, qualities and experience do you feel are most likely to impress the interviewers trying to fill this post?

4. Think about how you will convince them to appoint you

Ensure you can 'plug' yourself into the vacancy by quoting true-life examples of relevant lessons and experiences from your past career. Seek to show your skills and personal qualities in a positive light.

Let's suppose, for example, that the motor dealership you want to join as sales manager is going through the final stages of a difficult take-over. You might conclude that the company needs to appoint someone with experience of welding disparate teams together. You could then work out how best to convey the way you successfully tackled a similar situation – perhaps giving examples of how you exceeded your sales targets while simultaneously managing to improve staff morale. You might then come up with a practical idea or two of your own to show how you would push the combined business forward.

As you prepare, it's always a good idea to write out the kind of replies you would give to interview questions just as you would speak them – namely, in straightforward, conversational language. Think about how you would demonstrate each particular skill you believe the employer is looking for. For example:

From my time at XYZ Cars, I know all about the pitfalls of running two different sales incentive schemes. In my last job I was able to smooth things over with all the different people involved as we introduced a new system. I make a point of nurturing friendly relationships with staff at all levels. It's an important part of my job to be aware of anxieties staff may have. My boss valued me because of my ability to manage change.

I can see you need someone with good problem-solving skills here… When I started at ABC I was able to solve a lot of supply and delivery problems because of my good contacts in the industry. As well as managing my own team, I'm also used to dealing with directors who need information or answers at short notice.

I notice that while your forecourt is always spotlessly clean, the displays could have more impact and viewers may even not realize that they can walk through to inspect all the vehicles in the yard at the side. At ABC Motors I instigated a number of charity fun weekends and evening events, which raised sales by 32 per cent in six months, as well as getting us lots of great free publicity in the local media.

■ See if you can visit beforehand

It's well worth seeing if you can arrange a visit to the organization ahead of your interview. This gives you the chance to collect useful information, but will also help you to form your own opinions about the organization's activities and how it serves its customers. Your interest would almost certainly not go unnoticed by the recruiters, and you would leave their offices with a better mental picture of the prevailing culture and how you would (or would not) fit into it. Such a visit can be especially useful and reassuring if you are returning to work after a career break. You can also practise your journey and see for yourself how people tend to dress for work. Talking of which…

■ Dress the part

This might sound obvious, but a lot of people don't do it: dress for the job you're hoping to get. Clearly, different industries and professions have their own style identities, and you need to take that into account when you're choosing your interview clothes, but even for a job in a fashion-conscious sector, the general rule is to avoid anything extreme.

What you should be trying to do is present yourself as someone the interviewer can imagine actually doing the job you're going for. So if you're applying for a responsible role – say, finance director in an advertising agency – your clothes need to underpin your image as an intelligent executive who is capable of interacting with the wider business community, regardless of how the creative director may dress.

If you're working on the day of your interview, think about whether you need to take an alternative outfit to change into. Perhaps the role is more senior than the one you'll be dressed for, or in a sector with different ideas about workwear? The same is true if you're applying for a job within your own organization that might call for a different look: it may be appropriate to take other clothes to work in a suit carrier and change before your interview. The impression you make on an interviewer in the first few seconds of your meeting can be crucially important.

■ General rules about dress

- If you buy a new outfit for an interview, try it *all* on well beforehand (you need to feel comfortable in it, and you don't want to discover that your trousers need turning up on the morning of the meeting).
- When in doubt, lean more towards formal clothes than casual ones (even if everyone else is dressed down, your smart outfit will at least give the impression that you're taking the interview seriously).
- Even if fashion isn't your thing, make a point of dressing in a moderately contemporary style (you don't want your clothes to suggest that your attitudes in other areas might be old-fashioned or out of touch).
- Be wary of vivid colours (people can react very negatively to them).
- Avoid revealing too much flesh (employers worry about sexual harassment lawsuits).
- Avoid extreme make-up or hairstyles (unless the job you're going for demands a 'statement' look).
- Don't arrive looking crumpled, hot, wet or untidy in any way.
- Don't take more than a handbag or a briefcase into the meeting (with the obvious exception of presentation material or equipment, your coat and any other bags should be left with the receptionist).

- Pay close attention to hair, nails and personal hygiene (would you hire someone with body odour, sweat patches or dandruff?).
- Bad breath can be disastrous, so avoid strongly flavoured foods and alcohol for 24 hours beforehand.
- Avoid overpowering aftershave or perfume (scent is very subjective and can actively put people off you without them consciously knowing why).
- Avoid tobacco odours on your breath or clothes (now that workplaces are almost universally smoke-free, smoky smells can raise awkward questions in an interviewer's mind).
- Arrive 15 minutes early so that you can nip off to the cloakroom for last-minute hair-combing, tooth-brushing and outfit-checking (it's sod's law that this is the day you tuck your skirt into your knickers or sit on a piece of chewing gum on the bus).

■ Be aware of your mannerisms

You already know what sort of behaviour *you* would find off-putting or unsettling in others, so avoid all the following things yourself:

- A limp handshake – aim for firm rather than aggressive knuckle-crunching.
- Not making eye contact – though don't stare out the interviewer either.
- Poor posture – it makes you appear uninterested.
- Fidgeting – ditto.
- Speaking in an inaudible or overloud voice – match your tone to your interviewer's.
- Interrupting or finishing other people's sentences – plain irritating.
- Not being responsive enough – you need to play an active part and bat the ball back to the interviewer when you are given an opening.
- Negative speech patterns – use positive language, such as 'Yes, and…' instead of 'Yes, but…'

As for head-scratching, ear or lip-tugging, nail-nibbling or any other tic that involves touching your face – they all suggest indecision and/or lack of confidence, so avoid them.

We all have unconscious mannerisms. Ask your friends and family what yours are. Forewarned is forearmed.

Your main aim is to make the interviewer(s) warm to you so...

- Smile and look your interviewer in the eye when you first meet (easy to forget if you're tense).
- Let your expression and body language show that you're open to and interested in what is being said. Try not to cross your arms or appear defensive.
- At the end of the interview shake hands firmly, smile and thank the interviewers for their time.

■ Relaxation techniques

There are dozens of specialist books about relaxation, so if you know from experience that you find job interviews particularly stressful, it's probably worth your while to read one or two of them.

Alternatively, do the simple relaxation exercises described below. Try them out at home and, if you find them useful, do them before you set out for your interview. Handily, they're also discreet enough to be put into practice in that often nerve-racking period between arriving for your interview and waiting to be called into the meeting room.

CONTROLLED BREATHING

- Sit in a comfortable chair with good support for your back and head.
- Sit back in your chair with your feet on the ground and hands relaxed.
- Breathe in through your nose and be conscious of the air going right down to your stomach to the count of four.
- Hold the breath to the count of two.
- Release the breath through your mouth slowly to the count of six (with practice this could be extended to ten).
- Repeat three times.

Variation: When you feel comfortable about the breathing, alternate between concentrating on outside noises, smells and sensations for 30 seconds and switching your awareness to internal sensations and feelings (such as the air entering and leaving your body) for 30 seconds. This can induce a deeper sense of relaxation.

QUICK RELAXATION TECHNIQUES

- Say sharply to yourself, 'STOP'.
- Breathe in, hold your breath and slowly exhale, relaxing your shoulders.
- Pause for a moment, breathe in and out, relaxing your jaw and forehead.
- Pause for a moment, breathe in and out, relaxing your legs and feet.

And/or

- Pull in the stomach muscles tightly – hold for five – relax.
- Clench the fists tightly – hold for five – relax.
- Extend the fingers – hold for five – relax.
- Grasp below the seat of the chair – hold for five – relax.
- Press the elbows tightly into the sides of body – hold for five – relax.
- Push the feet hard into the floor – hold for five – relax.

And/or

- Sitting comfortably in a chair, close your eyes and imagine yourself to be transparent, filled with your favourite coloured liquid. Imagine it to be exactly at the temperature you find most comfortable.
- Starting at the crown of your head, imagine this liquid draining from your body. Imagine each part that is drained feels lighter, relieved of tension.
- Imagine the liquid eventually flowing out through the tips of your fingers and toes.

> **Source:** Adapted from the University of Liverpool Counselling Service website

■ Handling key questions

Most of the things you will be asked at your interview are likely to fall into three key areas: your *competency* to do the job, your *motivation* to do it, and whether you are a good *cultural fit* with the organization. Working out quickly what lies behind each question will help you to give a good answer.

- **Competency** questions usually arise from achievements you set out in your CV. In essence, why should the employer give you the job over someone else? You may be asked to describe a difficult situation you have faced at work and what you learnt from the experience. What's been your worst or proudest moment and why? How would you handle a given situation? What solutions do you have for the prospective firm's problems?

- **Motivation** questions try to discover how much you really want the job and how vigorously you will apply yourself to it. Questions could be along the lines of 'Why do you want to work for us?' You might also be asked what role you play in a team, how the job fits in with your ultimate career plan, or simply what aspects of the post interest you.
- **Cultural fit** questions seek to establish if you are 'one of us'. You may be asked what aspects of the organization you like or admire, or how you would describe your working or management style.

Turning weaknesses into strengths

One of the perennial and tricky questions that sometimes comes up is this one: 'What do you think is your main weakness?' You will need to be ready with a truthful answer, but always present it as positive rather than negative. For example, you might reply: 'My main weakness is being too enthusiastic. Sometimes I have to remind myself that others are not always as enthusiastic as I am. I need to bear their feelings in mind, and think of new ways to enthuse them.'

If you have been made redundant and are asked a direct question about the reason for leaving your job, it will be impossible to put a completely positive spin on what happened. However, don't dwell on the negatives. Stress that the loss of your post had nothing to do with your personal performance, and swiftly move the conversation on to how your experience equips you perfectly for the new job.

Don't panic if a question temporarily fazes you or puts you under stress. You might, for example, be asked a completely open question about how you would manage change, or if you are tough enough to take hard decisions. The interviewer is probably just testing how you would behave, so try to forearm yourself with a past work experience that you could use as an example.

It's a useful exercise to imagine the worst questions you could be asked – and to work out how would you reply to them. By comparison, the actual interview probably won't be nearly as bad!

Deliver your key message

No matter what questions they are actually asked by broadcast interviewers, politicians usually manage to make at least two or three predetermined points to back up their party's position. It's a technique worth copying. Work out and learn the most important and memorable things you want to say about why you are the best person for the job – and make sure you fit them into your answers. Remember too that all the best political speeches start and end strongly. When you sense that the interview is drawing to a close, try to leave the recruiter with a positive impression.

BE PREPARED

Time spent on preparation is never wasted, so why not try your hand at answering the following interview questions. You can write some notes on how you would answer them or, preferably, record them so that you can listen back to yourself and see how you sound. The questions are in no particular order, but they are all pretty standard, so the chances are that you will be asked at least some of them at every job interview you go for.

Don't try to learn your answers parrot-fashion. The aim of this exercise is simply to become clear in your mind about *what* you want to say (rather than the precise words you will use) so that you can produce a confident, informative yet succinct answer when the time comes.

- Tell me about yourself.
- What do you enjoy most about your current job?
- What is the biggest challenge you have faced at work?
- Why do you want to leave your current job?
- How do you see the role we're hoping to fill?
- Why do you think you would be suited for the role?
- Why do you want this job?
- Describe your working relationship with your existing boss.
- How much do you know about our company?
- Where do you see yourself in five years' time?
- What do you see as your greatest strengths?
- What would you say are your greatest weaknesses?
- How do you think your colleagues would describe you?
- If you were offered this job, how long would you expect to stay with the company?

■ Ask questions

Make sure you have at least a couple of good questions up your sleeve to ask at the end, if invited to do so. Don't sell yourself short by blurting out a dull question that could easily be answered by looking on the firm's website. Instead you might ask about some aspect of the job or organization that you have already thought about. Alternatively, you might question your interviewer about something that could influence your final decision to take the job, such as the longer-term prospects for promotion or overseas travel.

Yet another possible tactic is to ask what happened to the previous occupant of the job. The interviewer will expect something along these lines, and will respect you for asking. This approach may also help him or her to imagine you in the post. The more you can leave a final and lasting impression of you actually doing the job, the better.

■ Answer as if you're already in the job

One interview technique some coaches suggest is to imagine that you have already got the job. This is to encourage you to engage with the interviewer or panel or as if they were your new work colleagues. The idea is that if it were your first day in the new job, you would want to impress them and be liked, but you would also be more likely to ask intelligent questions and give less of a 'performance'.

One signal that the interviewer is interested in you might be asking what salary level you have in mind. Try not to be drawn into giving the smallest figure you would settle for. It's reasonable to ask for more time to negotiate your salary and benefits. Talk instead about your accomplishments and the financial value you would bring to the company. If you are forced to name a figure, be aware of what others in similar jobs are paid and add on some more. If the organization wants you, it will be ready to bargain.

■ Assessing an offer

Great! You've been offered the job. If you need the work, or you just can't wait to leave your current job, you will say, 'Yes. When do I start?' But what if you're not so sure? The key thing is that you don't have to make a decision on the spot, even if you get a job offer at the end of your interview. You should still give yourself time to run through a mental checklist first:

- Is the job a good fit for you? Check it against what you learnt about what you want out of your new career in Chapters 2, 5, 6, 8 and 9.
- Do you like the look of the place? Do you think you would enjoy spending your working day there?
- Do you feel positive about the people you've met there? Did they respond positively to you?
- Are there any questions you need to ask about your responsibilities, your boss, the team you'll be working with, and the support you'll get (including your induction, training and career progression)?
- Have you discussed and agreed *all aspects* of your remuneration package? When you're excited about being offered a job it's easy to overlook details such as benefits (pension, medical and life cover, company car), commission arrangements, bonuses, holiday allowance, staff appraisals and salary reviews.

If you're confident that this is the right job for you, fine – accept it, but don't leave the room without finding out when you can expect to receive a written offer detailing *everything* that you've agreed (and don't be tempted to resign from your existing job until you have that offer in your hand).

If you have any doubts about the job, thank the interviewer for the offer, ask for clarification of any outstanding issues in your mind and say that you'd like to take a little time (say, 24 hours) to consider it. Politely stick to your guns if you're pressed for an immediate answer.

If your request for thinking time is refused outright, you'll have to come up with some delaying tactics. Refusing time, however, would be an unusually aggressive tactic on the part of an employer, which would tell you something about the style of the organization. Say that you want to go to a coffee bar to think things over before giving a final decision. Undertake to return in an hour. Do your utmost to win some thinking time if you're not *completely sure* that this is the right job for you.

■ If you don't get the job…

The first thing to remember if you are not chosen is that it's not personal, so don't assume there's something wrong with you. There's often little to choose between the candidates who reach the last interview stage; in fact, the organization could well have agonized over the final decision. You don't take to everyone *you* meet, so you can't expect every employer to take a shine to you.

Likeability is, however, only one aspect of the selection process. The outcome rests as much on technical credentials, skills, track record in similar circumstances, personal chemistry and timing. Decisions are made by people whose own, unpredictable criteria may win out over the principles of fair selection. For example, the job may have gone to the nephew of someone who lives next door to the finance director.

If the interview was badly handled, or you felt it was conducted unprofessionally, comfort yourself with the thought that the company is unlikely to be a good employer.

■ Ask for feedback – and learn from it

Assess your handling of the interview objectively. Contact the interviewer or the HR department a few days after your rejection and ask directly in which areas they felt there was room for improvement, and what they felt you did right. This will help you to discover how you are coming across, and what you might do differently next time. If the organization is still on your hit list, stay in touch. Many firms will take a second look at people that they have already got to know. You may yet get a second chance to prove yourself.

■ Key points

- Many people fail to prepare thoroughly for each interview. Consider the exact job requirements, research the organization carefully, and draw closely on all the experience and skills you have gained to demonstrate how you would excel in the job.

- Most of the questions you will be asked will test one of three things: your *competency* to do the job, your *motivation* to do it, and whether you are a good *cultural fit* with the organization. Being able to recognize each kind of question will help you to give effective answers.

- Prepare about three key points to work into your responses. End on a positive note with a question of your own that will encourage the interviewer to imagine you doing the job for real.

- Ask for feedback if you don't get the job, and decide what you will do differently next time.

Smile, relax, and don't forget to make time for all those small conversations about nothing very important that oil the wheels of every workplace.

Chapter 16
You've got the job!

In this chapter you will find:

❑ Grooming

❑ Getting off to a good start

❑ Building relationships

S tarting a new job can be a very exciting and energizing time, particularly if you have been out of work or stuck in a role you dislike. But if you are getting back to work after a career break or a long stint with one employer, you may feel anxious that your unfamiliarity with twenty-first-century work practices will stick out a mile.

Boost your confidence before you start by setting aside some time to review everything you've learnt about the organization you're going to be working for. Revisit the website or reread any written information you have. Familiarize yourself with the products and services they provide. Search online for the latest information or news stories about the company and the sector. Memorize the names of the most senior people and those you'll be directly working with.

Think long and hard about how you're going to behave in your new job. Think about any mistakes you may have made in the past and work out how you will avoid repeating them in this job. Which areas do you need to read up on and concentrate on improving? Do they include any of the following?

■ Relationships with colleagues, superiors or subordinates.
■ Liaison and delegation skills.
■ Timekeeping and/or deadlines.
■ Prioritizing your workload.
■ Managing your career progression.
■ Dealing with clients and/or suppliers.

■ Review your wardrobe

We all know that we should not judge others by their appearance, but we all do it, and so will your new colleagues. The clothes you wear need to suit the style and image of both the organization you are joining and your new role. If you are not convinced that you have an adequate range of suitable outfits to get you through the first couple of weeks, go shopping.

You want to make a favourable impression on the people you will be meeting, so pay attention to your personal grooming: do not kid yourself that your colleagues won't spot unkempt fingernails, bad breath or a dandruff problem. The subliminal message projected by good grooming is efficiency and reliability, while an unkempt appearance suggests disorganization and an inability to cope.

So make time for a trip to the hairdresser, dentist or manicurist before you start your new job. And take some exercise – you'll feel and look better, and knowing that will boost your confidence.

■ Start well

You want to arrive in good time on your first day, feeling well rested and energetic, so avoid alcohol the previous evening and get a good night's sleep. If your mornings tend to be fraught because of family responsibilities, try to arrange for someone to give you a hand on your first morning so that you can concentrate on getting ready.

Make sure you know whom to ask for when you get to your new office. This is easy to forget and can land you in an embarrassing situation before you've even made it to your new desk.

■ Build good relationships

In the first few days and weeks it is vital to make the most positive impression you can on your boss and colleagues. This is the time when they will be making assessments about what sort of person you are and how you tend to behave, and the impressions they form tend to be long-lasting and difficult to change.

Regardless of how senior you'll be in your new role, you're more likely to make a favourable impression on your colleagues at all levels if you spend more time listening to them than talking at them in the first days and weeks. Tact and diplomacy should be your watchwords, showing that you're ready to be impressed rather than ready to criticize. Ask questions and call on colleagues for support, even if you're the new boss. If you behave as if you're on top of the job by the end of week one, you will only appear arrogant and antagonize people.

In stressful circumstances it can be easy to feel that everyone is judging you negatively, but this is unlikely to be true. Why would they when they have only just met you? Talk to your superiors and colleagues as often as you can, and try to gauge what sort of impression you're making and what their expectations are. Deal with any problems that crop up as calmly, positively and quickly as you can.

Don't fall into the trap of thinking that asking for help will be interpreted as a sign of weakness. If you do it in a relaxed way, it will actually make you appear confident and approachable.

■ Be nice

Be open to approaches from your colleagues. Say yes to offers of coffee, lunch and after-work drinks, even if you're busy, but avoid attaching yourself too closely to a clique or individual until you've thoroughly found your feet. Be wary of passing judgement on your predecessor's work, even if it quickly becomes clear to you that they were incompetent.

A lot of people will help you out one way or another in the first few days and weeks of a new job. Do not forget to thank them – they will really appreciate it.

■ Get to know your way around

Get to grips with the structure of the organization as quickly as you can: you need to know who's who and who does what. Explore the building and find out where the various departments and key individuals are located.

Familiarize yourself with how things are done: is this an open-door environment or an office where you need to negotiate access to senior people through their secretaries? Do people tend to talk through work issues round the water cooler or communicate via email? Is it a sociable workplace? Be cautious about suggesting new ways of doing things before you've established yourself, even if it's immediately obvious to you that improvements can be made.

■ Understand what you're being paid to do

Find out how your job fits into the wider organization, what your work priorities are, and what your superiors and colleagues expect from you. Establish the limits of your authority, whose time you can call on and who can call on your time. Make yourself aware of all the resources at your disposal and identify any sensitive or problem issues or people as soon as you can so that you can work out strategies to handle them.

■ Work a full day

Nothing will damage your reputation faster in the early days than turning up late in the morning, taking long lunches or leaving work too early. Whatever your contract says about the hours you are expected to work, if most of your colleagues work a longer day, take your cue from them and do the same – at least until you have got the measure of the place.

■ Enjoy yourself

Starting a new job can be exhausting. You have to take in a mass of new information, form relationships with a lot of people you've only just met, find your way around unfamiliar offices and systems, and get to grips with a different hierarchy – not to mention the inevitable quagmire of office politics. And, as if that weren't enough, you're conscious that you need to get on top of your job as fast as possible before your boss starts wondering if the right person has been appointed.

Calm down. It's more than likely that the performance standards you're setting yourself are far higher than your boss actually demands at this early stage. He or she knows that you need a grace period to settle in and that you are bound to make the odd mistake to begin with.

So don't exhaust yourself by working excessively long hours; instead, concentrate on working as *effectively* as possible. Time management is important, and if you don't know how to do it well, buy a book on the subject.

No one expects you to get on top of your job by the end of the first week, so smile, relax and don't forget to make time for those small conversations about nothing very important that oil the wheels of every workplace. You'll do fine.

■ Key points

- Do your homework before you start your new job: it will boost your confidence.
- Start to build good relationships with your colleagues as soon as possible.
- Do more listening than talking in the early days and weeks and keep any criticism to yourself.

The only human resources adviser or coach you can totally trust to look after your interests is you!

Chapter 17
How to be your own career coach

In this chapter you will find:

❑ The job rollercoaster

❑ Keeping sight of your goals

❑ Mentors and careers advisers

For anyone trying to raise their game at work, today's workplace may seem unforgiving and pressurized. It's tough to push out in a new direction when you've already taken on financial commitments and perhaps have a family or other dependents to support.

Yet the experience you may be going through now is one that millions have already faced. More to the point, many people who are currently as happy as Larry in their present jobs are about to find themselves in the same boat. So look on the bright side – you've actually got a head start!

The average time people spend in each single employment in the UK is now down to less than three years. Companies and organizations buy and sell each other, merge, restructure, upsize, downsize, rightsize, flourish and collapse. Even if we find a boss who takes an interest in encouraging, training and developing us, he or she will probably be gone within a couple of years.

What this means is that ultimately we all have to take personal responsibility for our own careers. The only human resources adviser or coach you can totally trust to look after your interests is you.

■ Careers go in all directions

Don't assume, even for a moment, that this present phase of job-searching and heart-searching will be your last. Those now starting work in their early 20s can expect to change their entire career or job field three times, and employer eight to ten times.

So how does anyone manage to get to the top – or even the middle – in today's unpredictable world of work? Well, think of it this way. The best way to climb a cliff isn't necessarily in a straight line. To make progress you may have to move sideways first. Our working lives are increasingly jumping around in the same way. Welcome to your zigzag career.

■ Moving sideways

Sideways moves were once regarded disparagingly as a sign that you were somehow failing to climb the corporate ladder. That view is clearly nonsense. Experience and variety are what counts, and with so few 'layers' of management left within organizations, few people can expect constant promotion.

The worst aspect of moving sideways is probably the discovery that your next job will be no better paid: indeed, you might find yourself worse off. But if you can prove that you have what it takes, your career may start going off in a more profitable new direction.

■ The job rollercoaster

Let's imagine that you work in administration. You have done well and find yourself managing ten people, but when your boss leaves, you are overlooked for promotion. To be honest, though, you realize you are bored with the work, which no longer stretches you. On a whim, you answer an advert and make a move to a much larger company. However, it's far from an impressive-sounding job, and the pay works out less once your transport costs are taken into account. At the new firm you are responsible for no one but yourself. Friends wonder if you have taken a step backwards. The tasks are more technical and you have to ask for lots of help, but your projects are completed so well that you soon get a pay rise and more responsibility.

You choose to make a series of sideways moves within the same company to broaden your experience, including two spells working abroad. Then, having had a great run for several years, disaster strikes. Your firm announces redundancies, and your job is among those being chopped. However, the redundancy money gives you a breathing space and you take a couple of months off. Fortunately, out of the blue, you run into a former client who knows your work and offers you a job on the strength of something you did for her years ago. This is a not untypical rollercoaster ride.

Over the years, you will resign from jobs or be laid off. You will have had promotions, demotions and numerous job titles, and have worked for many different bosses, good, bad and indifferent. People might work for you. Changing or even losing your role will be the catalyst to finding a new direction. All your experiences at work – positive and negative – have something valuable to teach you.

■ Swot your career!

Nobody quite knows who invented SWOT analysis, but since the 1960s, smart businesses have regularly reviewed their Strengths, Weaknesses, Opportunities and Threats. It's something we should all do with our own careers at least once a year. Here are some ideas to get you thinking.

■ **How can I play to my strengths?** Seek tasks where you can shine, and concentrate on deepening and extending skills in which you have the edge. Where do others feel that you excel?

■ **Can I tackle my weaknesses?** What do you do badly? For example, perhaps your communication or IT skills need brushing up. Ask your boss or trusted colleagues what you should be doing differently to get to the next level.

■ **Do I take every opportunity to raise my game at work?** Ask to go on courses or attend conferences to widen your horizons and knowledge. If necessary, offer to attend at your own expense and study further in your own time.

■ **What are the present or future threats to my current living?** Are business trends or changing technology or particular individuals threatening your position? If so, how can you reposition yourself now, while you have time?

As to what else you can do to kickstart your career prospects – well, don't forget to make your achievements known. This isn't showing off; it's marketing yourself – making sure the influential people in your organization know where you have personally 'added value'.

Whatever you do, don't allow yourself to be sucked into the negative carping that infects so many offices. Show instead that you are happy to embrace change. Champion more efficient working and be in the forefront of finding profitable new business or furthering your organization's goals.

■ Keep sight of your goals

Once you have found a new job, keep sight of the goals you set and ask yourself if you are still on track. You will need to work out for yourself when it's time to ask for more training, more responsibility or a pay rise.

People sometimes find it hard to admit that they have become bored with a job that once seemed so engaging. For example, demotivation may set in when you feel you don't have the freedom to do your work in the way you want to. Instead, you are being controlled by procedures or unthinking senior managers who keep checking up on you.

If you are to enjoy that particular job once again, the best approach may be to try to get your job reorganized so that you spend more time doing the aspects of it that you find most enjoyable and are best at. It's easy to be so absorbed in the day-to-day demands of work that you never get round to voicing your concerns and trying to approach the problem jointly with your employers.

Only you will know when it's time for a move once again. Don't be afraid. If you have changed your career once, you can do it again. Keep up to date with work trends and potential new opportunities with other organizations in your sector. You can manage your career or let it manage you.

■ Keep tabs on your network

We've talked about the importance of networking elsewhere in this book. Never overlook the value of keeping in touch with people you meet at work-related or social functions. These contacts may be able to.

- Advise you about a particular company or industry.
- Give you job leads.
- Introduce you to others so that you can expand your own network.

It's important to keep in touch with your contacts. Find excuses to have friendly chats when you can casually keep tabs on what's going on in their particular areas. Most people enjoy helping others, and you may soon be able to help them in return.

And don't waste all this effort by being disorganized and discovering that you have lost a vital phone number, email address or business card. Use a computer address book or contacts software to record names, titles, addresses and contact details, and keep detailed notes of when you spoke and what ideas or projects you discussed. The wider your network of contacts, the more potential opportunities you will know about. One day one such opportunity could be just right for you.

■ Look for a mentor

Sometimes networking can help you in an unexpected way by providing you with a mentor – someone outside your immediate circle who can be an independent and trusted guide and adviser. Mentors act as sounding boards to help people become more effective or to help them decide what they want to do as they progress in their careers. To find a mentor, look for someone you admire and respect. A mentor need not be much older than you, but it should be someone with whom you get on well. Ideally, it's also someone with connections, who is in a position you'd like to be in one day. Don't choose your boss – you want to be able to speak freely!

Mentors are most likely to say 'yes' to working with you if you remind them of themselves in some way. Agree at the start that you can end the relationship with no hard feelings on either side if it doesn't work out: you may need to extricate yourself politely if you don't feel comfortable with each other, or if your mentor proves too judgemental or controlling. Look for someone with a positive and upbeat attitude, and try to meet regularly – say, once every couple of months or so.

How mentors can help

Your mentor should be someone you can bounce ideas off – someone who can provide you with a fresh perspective on your career and workplace problems. He or she can help you to assess your strengths and weaknesses, as well as to develop skills for success and a long-range career plan. If you share the same employer, your mentor can also help you to navigate your organization's culture and politics.

Mentors can help you to question your reasons for doing something, and to avoid learning lessons the hard way. They can dispel myths, give practical tips on applying for work or going for interviews, and help you to make sense of your choices. They may be able to shed light on the apparently strange or unpredictable behaviour of colleagues or managers you encounter because mentors have usually seen it all before.

■ Life coaches

If you feel you need outside help, but can't find a suitable mentor, you might consider working with a life coach. A good one specializing in career counselling should be able to help you work out your priorities and devise an action plan to address your weaknesses. Life coaches use numerous techniques drawn from sociology and psychology. The most widely recognized professional accreditation body for personal and business coaches is the International Coach Federation (**www.coachfederation.org.uk**). The 'Hiring a Coach: individuals' section of the website has some useful pointers. Also see the FAQ section of **www.achievementspecialists.co.uk**.

■ Careers advisers

Further help in working towards your career goals can also be obtained from careers advisers. Most use psychometric, personality, IQ and other tests to help you define your core skills. It's likely you'd have a limited number of meetings with a careers adviser, whereas the length of your relationship with a life coach will depend on the range and complexity of the goals you agree between you (some of which may not directly relate to your work).

Career counselling accreditation is offered by several bodies, including:

British Association for Counselling (BAC) – **www.bac.co.uk**

British Psycholological Society (BPS) – **www.bps.org.uk**

Institute of Careers Guidance (ICG) – **www.icg-uk.org**

If you are paying for the service, make sure you check the counsellor's qualifications.

■ Think before you buy

Without wishing to denigrate the work of the many reputable careers advisers and coaches, always do your research carefully before you shell out for advice. There is a vast array of services available, most of which play mercilessly on the natural insecurity people feel when they are trying to find a new direction. Such organizations charge fees that may range from a few pounds to literally thousands, and provide advice that may be at best general, and at worst unhelpful. That said, there's also plenty of good careers help to be found online, so do try all the free stuff first.

■ Key points

- With people spending only three years or so in each employment, we will all have to learn to take responsibility for our own career progression.
- For many, this may mean taking a pay cut or making a sideways move to go off in a new direction as the job market changes.
- Everyone should take a cool and regular look at their job situation to ensure they are playing to their strengths, addressing personal weaknesses, taking up new opportunities and evaluating future threats to their position.
- Find a mentor and build a network of contacts in your field. Their advice and support will be invaluable to you in your future career.

Make a commitment to overcome whatever barriers stand in your way – and stick to it.

18
You can do it!

In this chapter you will find:

❏ Self-belief

❏ Life after redundancy

❏ Momentum is everything

As a career-changer, it's natural to feel powerless at times. You are not in command of other people's time, their priorities or their decisions. You know you have to make contacts and sell yourself, even though you may not feel confident or comfortable about doing that. But you can do it – and the results will be worth it.

You're not alone. Job-changing is now so commonplace that all of us are having to change our ideas about what constitutes a 'good career'. Like it or not, work will never be the same again: people increasingly switch job fields, functions and industries; employment in private and public organizations will continue to wax and wane as the global economy brings both new opportunities and threats. More people will go part-time, work on contract, become self-employed, or assemble a 'portfolio' career to earn their living. So think of your career as a journey you will take over the course of your working life, not a destination in itself.

■ No more self-delusion

Try listing all the old excuses you find yourself trotting out to explain why you are stuck in a job rut – all those so-called 'reasons' that are holding you back from a better career. Here's a selection:

■ I can't think of anything else to do.
■ I'm rubbish at interviews.
■ My skills are outdated.
■ I can't take rejection.
■ I have health problems.
■ I can't use a computer.
■ I can't travel far.
■ I'm too old/young.
■ It would be too difficult to retrain.
■ I have no confidence.

None of these things are valid reasons to hold you back from moving into a career where you can flourish. Think back over your life and you will see that there have been times when you did manage to rise above difficulties like these, and worse. You can do it again. Make a commitment to overcome whatever barriers stand in your way – and stick to it.

■ Life after redundancy

If you've been made redundant and are having trouble making progress, it is almost certainly because you are carrying 'emotional baggage' left over from things that happened at work in the past. Stop brooding on past events: you cannot change a thing about them. Instead, start focusing your energies on your future. Talk things through with someone you trust. Take that old job label off yourself. Your last job may have somehow conferred status or a particular image, but it never defined you as an individual.

Everybody who is 'resting' between jobs dreads that awkward question at parties: 'So what do you do?' Seriously consider finding some voluntary work to get you back into the swing of things and give you valuable experience and contacts you can use in the future. One of the most important assets you have is your self-esteem. Do not neglect it. Discover ways to keep it high and you will find it easier to handle your career change with confidence and a sense of purpose.

■ Momentum is everything

What do you think is the single biggest obstacle between you and a great new job? The answer is...you. If you really want to find work that you love, you have to devote yourself to the career-change process. Putting in a few hours a week will not be enough. If you are not working, you will need to dedicate at least as much time as you would expect to spend in paid employment. Give each job-hunting day some structure, set yourself goals and stick to them. What background information do you need and where will you get it from? How many named individuals and organizations will you contact before the end of the day? What calls will you make or follow up? Whom will you meet?

The good news is that some of the best career moves are made after a period of introspection and uncertainty. Jobs are always out there. Employment success stories are all around us. It's never too late for anyone to discover or train for the kind of work that will suit them better. Changing your career may not be easy and the process may take longer than you hoped. But you *can* do it, and it *will* be worth it. What are you waiting for?

Useful websites

Here, as a quick reminder, are the websites we refer to within the text.

Age Concern: www.ageconcern.co.uk

Apprenticeships: www.apprenticeships.org.uk

Business Link: www.businesslink.gov.uk

Career guidance in Scotland: www.careers-scotland.org.uk

Career guidance in Wales: www.careers-wales.com

Career/personality matching: http://online.onecenter.org

Citizens Advice Bureau: www.citizensadvice.org.uk

City & Guilds exams: www.cityandguilds.com

Consumer Credit Counselling Service: www.cccs.co.uk

Counselling accreditation: British Association for Counselling (BAC)
    www.bapc.co.uk; British Psychological Society (BPS) www.bps.org.uk;
    Institute of Careers Guidance (ICG) www.icg-uk.org

Countryside Jobs Service: www.countryside-jobs.com

Courses: www.learndirect-advice.co.uk/findacourse

Debt restructuring: www.adviceguide.org.uk; www.citizensadvice.org.uk

Employers Forum on Age: www.efa.org.uk

Employer's Guide to Training Providers: www.lsc.gov.uk

Entrepreneurs: www.thebigtrip.co.uk

Financial Services Authority: www.fsa.gov.uk/consumer

Graduate careers advice: www.careers.lon.ac.uk/SORTIT; www.fish4.co.uk/
    iad/jobs; www.prospects.ac.uk

IT jobs: www.computing.co.uk

Jobs4U Careers Database: www.connexions-direct.com

Job searching: www.jobcentreplus.gov.uk; www.worktrain.gov.uk

Job 'tasting': www.vault.com

Key skills: www.bbc.co.uk/skillswise

Life coaches: www.coachfederation.org.uk; www.achievementspecialists.co.uk

Medical jobs: doctorjob.co.uk

Motivation: www.mentalhelp.net/psyhelp

Myers-Briggs analysis: http://tools.monster.com/perfectcareer/

National Debtline: www.nationaldebtline.co.uk

Networking events: www.supper-club.net

NextStep: www.nextstep.org.uk

Organizational culture: www.careerleader.com/sstn/culture-test.html

Pension Service: www.thepensionservice.gov.uk

Personal profiling: www.learndirect-advice.co.uk/helpandadvice/dmr/; www.peoplemaps.co.uk

Pharmaceutical and healthcare jobs: www.inpharm.com

Prospects: www.prospects.ac.uk

Relate: www.relate.org.uk

Skill assessment: www.learndirect-futures.co.uk; http://online.onecenter.org/

Starting out: www.starttalkingideas.org; www.businesslink.gov.uk; www.dti.gov.uk; www.princes-trust.org.uk; www.shell-livewire.org

Suiting learning to lifestyle: www.direct.gov.uk/EducationAndLearning/AdultLearning

Time planning: www.bbc.co.uk/learning/returning/learninglives/time